Also by JOSEPH FIELDS

DOUGHGIRLS

With Jerome Chodorov
JUNIOR MISS

MY SISTER EILEEN

WONDERFUL TOWN

THE PONDER HEART

ANNIVERSARY WALTZ

With Anita Loos
GENTLEMEN PREFER BLONDES

Also by PETER DE VRIES

NO BUT I SAW THE MOVIE

THE TUNNEL OF LOVE

COMFORT ME WITH APPLES

THE TUNNEL OF LOVE

The Tunnel of Love

By JOSEPH FIELDS

and PETER DE VRIES

A Play
BASED UPON THE NOVEL
BY PETER DE VRIES

❧

Little, Brown and Company · BOSTON · TORONTO

Photographs by courtesy of Friedman-Abeles

CAST

AUGIE POOLE	Tom Ewell
ISOLDE POOLE	Nancy Olson
DICK PEPPER	Darren McGavin
ALICE PEPPER	Elisabeth Fraser
ESTELLE NOVICK	Sylvia Daneel
MISS MC CRACKEN	Elizabeth Wilson

The play was presented by The Theatre Guild on the night of February 13, 1957, at the Royale Theatre, New York. The play was directed by Joseph Fields, the production designed and lighted by Ralph Alswang, and Philip Langner was production associate.

The action takes place in Westport, Connecticut, in the studio of Augie Poole — a converted barn.

ACT I

ACT II

ACT III

ACT ONE

ACT ONE

Scene One

SCENE: *The scene is* AUGIE POOLE'S *studio, near Westport, Connecticut, which also serves as a living room and bar for relaxation and entertaining. It is a converted barn joined to a small house, a large cheerful place with a high-beamed ceiling and big windows that look out on a rolling country- side, lush and green in mid-June. The furnishings are cov- ered in bright chintz, and there is an alcove up one step at the left side where* AUGIE *works, containing a large drawing board and a hodgepodge of artists' materials. A door up- stage center serves as a separate entrance to the studio from the road. Another door, down right, leads into the house proper. There's a small bar left, with two stools in front of it. A sofa is left center, with a small table behind it. Another small table stands at the end of the bar with one of of those phones with a speaker attachment. A door up left leads into the guest bathroom. Several posters are on the wall, of past art shows by Picasso, Leger, Braque, and others. There is a bassinet outside near the center window. A bench is over right. The over-all effect is early New Eng- land cross-pollinated with Frank Lloyd Wright, on an inex- pensive scale.*

AT RISE: *We find four people caught in a visibly high point in their lives. Standing left dramatically is* ISOLDE POOLE, *a beautiful girl in her late twenties. She is rigid*

3

with indignation, her eyes flashing. DICK *and* ALICE PEPPER, *looking distraught, are center and up center respectively.* DICK *is a man in his late thirties, handsome and normally very self-assured.* ALICE *is about the same age as* ISOLDE, *attractive in a dim sort of way, wearing her usual costume — an anticipation blouse over a loose skirt. She's about three months on the way at this time. Off at one side, near the bar, stands* AUGIE POOLE, *looking like the social leper he feels at the moment.* AUGIE *is thirty or so, a permanent pixy, whose usual sardonic expression has turned to harrowed bewilderment.*

ALICE

But, darling, you're not being fair. You're condemning the poor boy without giving him a chance —

ISOLDE

(*Scathingly*)

He had his chance and he took it!

ALICE

That's unfair, darling. How can you condemn a man on circumstantial evidence?

AUGIE

(*Suffering*)

Alice, please. I know you mean well, but for the love of God stop defending me.

(*Desperately*)

Isolde, give me ten minutes alone with you first. Please —

ISOLDE

No! I'm getting out! I'm sick of you and Westport and everybody in it!

AUGIE

Where are you going?

ISOLDE

I don't know, but it'll be a city — any city!
(*She crosses to door right and turns*)
I never want to see a tree, or a blade of grass, or a piece of chintz again as long as I live!
(*She goes out. They stand staring at the door for a moment*)

DICK
(*Turns to* AUGIE, *trying to be hopeful*)
She's exaggerating.

ALICE
(*To* AUGIE)
I can see why she hates *you*, but why blame it on Westport?
(AUGIE *pays no attention*)

DICK

Augie, she doesn't mean all those things. For her own self-respect she had to blow her top, but she'll get over it.
(AUGIE *doesn't look at them*)

5

ALICE

I always thought Isolde was deep, but now I see that deep down she's shallow.

(DICK *looks at her*)

DICK

(*Murmurs*)
Um — "deep down she's shallow . . ."
(*Then to* AUGIE, *crossing*)
Augie, maybe it's a good thing this has happened. Only a storm could clear so foul a sky.
(*Puts his arm on* AUGIE's *shoulders*)
Why don't you come over to our place tonight? We'll have dinner and map out a plan of action.

AUGIE

(*Shrugging arm off shoulder*)
Thanks. Do me a favor and stay away from me with your damn plans.

DICK

(*Hurt*)
That's right, turn on *me*. I should've known better.

ALICE

Don't attack Dick because you hate yourself.

AUGIE

I hate both of us.

6

DICK
(*Nobly*)
Very well, Augie. If you decide you ever need a friend again, just pick up the phone —

AUGIE
Friend? What did you ever do for me? I'll tell you what. Loused me up with my wife and destroyed me as an artist, that's what.

DICK
Come on, dear, let's go home.
(*DICK and ALICE go to door*)
Let's leave him alone, so he can reach down into his ego and battle it out with his id.

ALICE
(*As they go out*)
Oh, stop using big words.
(*The door closes*)

AUGIE
Battle it out with my id. Silly bastard.
(*He crosses behind bar and pours a stiff straight drink*)
For years you struggle; just when you get your head above water they pull the rug from under you. . . . It figures.
(*He lifts his eyes to heaven*)
Up there they look down and say, "How's Augie Poole getting along?" "Oh, he's doing fine." "Is that so? Let's slug him!" "What'll

7

we do, Boss? Break his arm so he can't draw?" "No, he can't draw anyway." "Give him a concussion?" "No, he hasn't a brain in his head." "*I* know what we'll do. We'll break up his home — and if that doesn't do it, we'll do something drastic."

(AUGIE *looks up*)

Thanks, boys, that did it.

(*He drinks, then crosses right, almost tearful*)

Isolde darling, no matter what you think, I love you . . . I know that sounds pretty feeble after everything that's happened, but it's not my fault. I'm just a night moth, battering at the screen door of the inscrutable. We're all children, sliding down the banister of eternity.

(*Shrugs*)

I wish I knew what the hell I was talking about. Isolde, ask yourself — how did this all happen? If you'd only listen to me I could trace it back for you. . . . That day, about a year ago — I remember it because it was our fifth anniversary, and I forgot it . . .

(*He drinks again*)

COMPLETE BLACKOUT

(*Lights come up. It's a bright summer day. The room is empty. The door is open. After a moment* ALICE *enters, followed by* DICK. *He carries a champagne bucket containing three bottles of champagne, and a potted philodendron plant.*)

8

DICK

Anybody home?
(*He places plant on table behind sofa and carries bucket to bar.* ALICE *goes to door right and calls*)

ALICE

Isolde! Isolde! — Nobody.

DICK

Five years. . . . What were we doing on our fifth anniversary?
(*He is arranging champagne and tying ribbon. Ribbon has "Happy Fifth Anniversary" printed on it*)

ALICE

(*Humorously grim*)
I don't know what *you* were doing, but I was being wheeled into the delivery room, as usual.

DICK

You were? Oh, sure — Maude.

ALICE

Not Maude — *Ralph.*

DICK

(*Embarrassed*)
Ralph . . . I *meant* Ralph.
(*Behind her back he shrugs, finishes tying ribbon*)

9

ALICE

(*Sighs*)

I miss the kids. I know camp's the best place for them, but I miss them terribly, don't you?

DICK

(*Cheerfully*)

Not a damn bit.

(*Takes cigarette from bar*)

ALICE

Dick!

DICK

I'm sick of their sibling revelry.

ALICE

Sibling rivalry.

DICK

Same thing.

(*He lights cigarette*)

ALICE

Life is so ironic. Here we are having our fourth and they're trying so hard to have a baby. She's taking her temperature every day, keeping fever charts, going to the doctor, taking fertility tests, and driving herself crazy.

DICK

She's driving Augie a little crazy too.

ALICE

All he has to do is keep on tap at the right time. That's nothing.

DICK

Oh, that's nothing to you, huh?

ALICE

And you who resent your family, all you have to do is look at me. It's ironic.

DICK

Yes, it is — but we can't keep it up. Three kids and another one on deck. Nobody's got that kind of money.

ALICE

You don't seem to realize how much I've saved you on clothes alone.

(DICK *turns to drawing board and looks at it idly*)

If you got a few bills from Bergdorf's instead of the Anticipation Shop you'd know.

DICK

(*Chuckles*)

This is damn good!

ALICE

(*Taking jelly beans from dish on coffee table*)

What is?

DICK

(*Picks up a cartoon*)

This cartoon Augie's working on. . . . Two missionaries in a cannibal pot about to be cooked. One missionary says to the other: "At least our work hasn't been in vain. They're going to say grace."

(*He replaces cartoon.* AUGIE *comes into the studio looking very hot and weary, carrying a large portfolio. He leans on door*)

AUGIE
(*Seeing them, a little surprised*)

Oh, hello —

DICK

Augie!

ALICE
(*Goes to him, kisses him*)

Hi, Augie! Congratulations.
(*He looks puzzled*)
Happy Anniversary!

AUGIE
(*Wearily*)

Thanks — thanks.

DICK

Yes, boy, congratulations. You look terrible.

AUGIE

I *feel* terrible.

ALICE

Bad in town, huh?

12

AUGIE

It was a hundred and five. And I missed my train. When I finally got one I couldn't get a seat. And the air conditioning on the lousy New Haven club car was off. I guess somebody took that ice cube out of the ventilator and put it in a drink. This was one of those days when if I'd stood in bed the plaster would have fell. But if a man can smile and dust himself off, and stick out his chin and keep coming back for more — well, sir, show me that man and I'll show you a goddam fool.

DICK

Why did you pick a day like today to go in?

AUGIE

(*Leans portfolio in alcove under shelf*)

I had an appointment at the New Yorker. And when I got there the rat had flown to London.

(*He picks up letter from shelf*)

What do you hear from your kids?

ALICE

Oh, we get their weekly postcards.

DICK

"Dear Pop — got poison ivy — send money — send money — "

AUGIE

(*Smiles, hands letter to* DICK *who passes it on to* ALICE)

I got a long letter from Ralphie. He's on the swimming team. Wonderful kid!

13

ALICE

You'll let us know if he gets sick or anything.

AUGIE

(*Looks around*)

Where's Isolde? She didn't meet me at the station and there were no cabs, so I had to walk.

ALICE

Maybe she's at the doctor's.

AUGIE

(*Nods, crossing to phone*)

She spends half her life there.

(*He presses a button without taking off the hook and dials five numerals*)

DICK

What the hell is that?

AUGIE

(*Proudly*)

A new gadget I just got. Watch.

(*He leans on window looking out nonchalantly. A* VOICE *comes over loudspeaker*)

VOICE

Doctor Vancouver's office.

AUGIE

Is Mrs. Poole there?

VOICE

No, she isn't. Not today.

AUGIE

(*Still looking out window*)
When she gets there, Miss Watkins, tell her that fellow she
lives with down on Whortleberry Road is waiting home for her.
(*He switches it off*)
Isn't that great? I don't have to hold the phone. Now I can keep
drawing and talk at the same time.
(*Sees champagne bucket*)
Where'd that come from?

DICK

From us.

ALICE

(*Points to plant*)
That, too! I'm afraid it'll never grow, the jardiniere's too small.
It's going to be potbound.

AUGIE

This is damn nice of you both. And thanks for reminding
me. . . . Wish I felt more like celebrating . . . but I've been so low
lately . . .
(*He picks up cartoon and looks at it sadly.* DICK *follows
his gaze*)

DICK

That's a damn funny idea, Augie.

AUGIE

(*Eyes him*)
But you don't like the drawing?

15

DICK

(*Uneasily*)

Oh, sure — sure I do.

AUGIE

But not enough for the *Townsman* to buy it?

DICK

Look, my boy, I'm not an art critic, I'm an editor. And an editor is merely a panderer who brings the artist and his public together. That's what I'm trying to do — so why don't you break down and sell us your ideas and then instead of being an artist who doesn't sell his work, you'll be an idea man who *does*.

AUGIE

"Idea man." Euphemism for "gag man." Is that my fate? Gag man? Turning out jokes for other artists to draw?

DICK

(*Quickly*)

I think of you as a social satirist, like George Bernard Shaw.

AUGIE

(*Grimly*)

Sure, Shaw was a helluva cartoonist.

(*Disgustedly*)

Alice, take him home, will you?

ALICE

(*Crosses up center*)

Come on, Dick. Call us when Isolde gets back. Come on, honey.

DICK

I'll be there in a minute, dear.

ALICE

Try not to get loaded, will you, Big Daddy?
(*She goes out.* DICK *looks after her, then goes to phone and dials five numbers*)

DICK

Mind if I use your phone?

AUGIE
(*Waves wearily*)

A rhetorical question.

DICK

This call is private.
(*A* VOICE *booms over loudspeaker*)

VOICE

Westport Arms.

DICK
(*Jumps*)

Hey! How do you switch this thing off?

AUGIE

Third button.

DICK
(*Pushes button and sits in swivel chair*)

Miss Terry McBain, please . . .

(*He smiles at* AUGIE, *who gives him a look and shakes his head*)

Hello, Terry? Dick . . . fine. . . . How do you like the room? Comfortable? . . . Good! Look, Terry, I find that I'll be free this afternoon, so why don't I come over and we can discuss your libretto? I got a couple of good ideas since yesterday. . . . Did you bring your record player with you? I got the new Scarlatti Pastorale in G major.

(*He chuckles*)

A tuta lors.

(*He hangs up*)

Thanks, pal.

AUGIE

A lady librettist, eh?

DICK

She's a lovely thing. Just to look at her sends the blood coursing through my veins.

AUGIE

In contrast to the usual route it takes.

DICK

(*Jauntily, crossing to center*)

I'll see you later, my boy, I have a very intellectual afternoon ahead of me. We're going to discuss the position of the artist in modern society.

AUGIE

Aren't you taking an awful chance bringing her up here?

18

DICK

Uh-huh. Makes it more exciting.

AUGIE

I don't understand you. A lovely wife, three kids, another one on the way — and you're always on the prowl. Why? What for?

DICK

Righteous moral indignation ill becomes you, Augie, my boy.

AUGIE

I'm not being righteous — I just don't get it.

DICK

How could you? You've never heard the call of the Great Unknown.

AUGIE

(*Waves him off, disgustedly*)
Go on, music lover — answer the call.

DICK

It's simple for you to talk. You don't have the same ego drives. You're too damn normal.

AUGIE

I resent that!

DICK

Of course you are . . .
(*His eye falls on plant*)
You're like that plant — you need more elbow room — more dirt — a bigger jardiniere! You'll never be an artist because

19

you're denying yourself the emotional soil your roots need. You're *potbound!*

AUGIE

And you — you're a screwed-up Luther Burbank! You just attacked me for being too normal. A perfect example of double-think.

(*Sits on sofa*)

DICK

One thing doesn't contradict the other. Almost *all* normal people are inhibited.

AUGIE

(*Stretches out on sofa*)
Hold it, Doctor. Let me get comfortable.

DICK

There is nothing as smug as a monogamous man!
(*Car horn sounds cheerily outside.* DICK *crosses to bar*)
Mind if I have a drink?

AUGIE

Another rhetorical question!
(ISOLDE *enters wearily, dressed in town clothes. She carries a box which she places on bench with her purse*)

ISOLDE

Oh, Augie, I'm dead!

AUGIE

You are, huh?

20

ISOLDE

Hi, Dick!

DICK

Hi!

(*He sits on bar stool*)

ISOLDE

I'll never take the car into town again!
(*Crosses to sofa, kisses* AUGIE *on cheek*)
You were smart to take the train.

AUGIE

I wasn't smart. *You* got the car first.

ISOLDE

Well, it was absolutely useless. I couldn't even get into a parking lot — so I just left it in front of Bonwit's.
(*She hands him a traffic ticket*)
Here.

AUGIE

Thanks.
(*Reads it thoughtfully*)
"Unlawful Parking." On Fifth Avenue?
(*He sits up*)
Twenty-five bucks.

21

ISOLDE

I'm terribly sorry, darling, but *you* wanted to live in the country. Not I.

AUGIE

(*Nods*)
So I deserve the ticket. That's logical.

ISOLDE

(*Lays car keys on coffee table*)
Here are your keys. Anyway, I found just what I wanted. I bought a dress at Bonwit's — a lovely watermelon shantung.

AUGIE

Fine. Now you have something fit to wear into Saks.
(ALICE *comes in center and goes to* ISOLDE)

ALICE

Happy Anniversary, darling!

DICK

Congratulations.

ISOLDE

(*Looks at* DICK, *back to* ALICE. *It dawns on her*)
Oh — oh, thanks, dearest.

AUGIE

Oh, so you forgot it. Okay, it's a stand-off.

ALICE

(*Looks at box*)
Did you find anything?

AUGIE

(*Rises*)

Yes. A watermelon shantung and a ticket on the windshield.

DICK

Look, I've got to run — some important business in the village.
(*Makes false start. Stopped by* ISOLDE)

ISOLDE

Oh, wait a minute, Dick —
(*She goes to* AUGIE *and links her arm with his, smiles radiantly*)
— we have something to tell you and Alice — something exciting!

ALICE

(*Very eagerly*)

You *have?* What?

ISOLDE

(*Self-consciously*)

It's just that — we're going to enlarge our family.

DICK

Great!

ALICE

Isolde! How long have you known?

AUGIE

(*Quickly*)

It's not that. We're going to adopt one.

23

ALICE
(*Deflated*)

Oh . . .

DICK

Is *that* all?

AUGIE

All?

(*He shrugs*)
Yeah — I guess having a baby isn't much in *your* life.

DICK
(*Nods*)
Alice can have a baby at the drop of a hat.

AUGIE
(*Shrugs. Half to himself*)
I don't even own a hat.

DICK

Well, well! — Boy or girl?

AUGIE

Not so fast. We only put our names in a few days ago.

ISOLDE
(*Crosses to* ALICE)
At Rock-a-bye — that agency where the Marshalls got theirs.

ALICE

Where is that agency?

24

ISOLDE

New Haven.

AUGIE

We can stop off at Yale and enroll him in the Class of '79.
(*He reflects*)
My God, what won't the tuition be then!

ALICE

(*To* ISOLDE)
Darling, I think it's just wonderful — wonderful!

ISOLDE

(*To* ALICE)
I hope you don't mind — we gave you and Dick as references.

ALICE

Mind? We're delighted! Aren't we, Dick?

DICK

You bet! Delighted!

ALICE

You'll make ideal parents. Our kids are crazy about you.

ISOLDE

(*Nods*)

Especially Augie.

DICK

Sure — he plays with them. If they weren't mine *I'd* play with them too.

ISOLDE

(*Turning to* AUGIE)
Isn't it exciting? I can hardly wait.

AUGIE

(*Warningly*)
Now take it easy, darling, they have thousands of applications for babies, and every one of them has to be investigated first. They'll get around to us, but it may take a little time.

ALICE

Now, does this mean you're giving up the tests?

ISOLDE

Oh no, we're trying everything! We're going to exhaust every possibility.
(AUGIE *looks at* DICK *who raises glass and grins broadly. Suddenly, anxious*)
Say, what time is it?

ALICE

Five o'clock.

ISOLDE

Oh! I almost forgot. My chart!
(*She runs into house*)

ALICE

If we're going to be investigated, maybe we'd all better cut down on the late parties and drinking.

DICK

Investigated? I never realized a thing like that could happen in this country. You mean they might be checking up behind our backs, without our knowing it?

AUGIE

Of course. They'll assign a case worker to us — a woman with her hair skun back in a bun and a mouth like a mail slot — a typical American Gothic — and leave us ask ourselves what virtues she'll want to find in the prospective parents and their cosigners. First, stability; then, solvency; next, sobriety; and finally — chastity.

(*He looks at* DICK *significantly*)

DICK

(*Indignantly*)

Why must people go around looking for fleas in one another's hides, like monkeys? Western culture — the way it mauls and mangles the individual for society! I say it's time we turned it around and organized society for the individual! It's un-American!

ALICE

Oh, shut up, Dick.

(*Turns to* AUGIE)

I just hate it when he starts to talk like that. You could start cutting down right now.

(*She picks up dress box and* ISOLDE's *purse and goes to door right. She turns*)

Skip one!

(*She exits.* DICK *drinks*)

AUGIE

She's right. You'd better start making yourself over into a good reference.

(DICK *starts to drink*)

And not just liquor. You're going to have to do something about your sex life.

DICK

What the hell are you trying to do, liquidate me? Now I've got to change *my* personal life so you'll make a good father!

AUGIE

(*Quickly*)

Look, if you'd like us to withdraw your name, we will.

DICK

(*Shrugs*)

No — I made my point and I'll submit to the inevitable. Modern man is a Laocoön, writhing in the red tape that strangles us all.

(*Drinks and to center*)

Dammit, you've ruined my afternoon; you've touched my quivering conscience and got me out of the mood. I'll call my date off.

AUGIE

(*Sardonically*)

What's another moosehead over the fireplace in your life? Thanks, boy.

THE TUNNEL OF LOVE

DICK

(*Sets glass on table behind sofa*)

See you later? We're going to the poetry reading and barbecue at the Marshalls'.

AUGIE

Hot dogs and Dylan Thomas. No, thanks. I'm beat. I haven't the strength to do anything.

(*Stretches out on sofa*)

All I want to do is take a cold shower and get into bed.

DICK

Well, okay. Give me a ring if you change your mind.

(*He exits, leaving door open.* ALICE *and* ISOLDE *enter from house.* ISOLDE *is wearing blue jeans, man's blue shirt with tail hanging out, and sneakers. She is carrying the chart and thermometer*)

ALICE

(*In a tone of repressed excitement*)

I'll see you later. Now you call me the minute you know anything.

ISOLDE

I'll phone you as soon as we get back.

(ALICE *hurries out, closing door.* ISOLDE, *very excited, crosses to* AUGIE)

AUGIE

What is all this?

ISOLDE

I just called Dr. Vancouver's office. He said to get hold of you right away! It's *up!*

AUGIE

Huh? What's up?

ISOLDE

My temperature!

AUGIE

(*Uneasily*)

Oh . . . it is, huh.

ISOLDE

(*Kneeling to show him graph*)

Yes! See here on the chart? You can follow the graph, see the way that line goes up?

AUGIE

Uh-huh.

ISOLDE

(*Excitedly, rising*)

Come on, Augie. Dr. Vancouver's only going to wait for us till six o'clock.

AUGIE

Huh?

ISOLDE

(*Impatiently*)

Oh, don't be so dense, Augie! You saw the chart! This is the *day!*

AUGIE

Ohhh — it is, huh?

ISOLDE

Yes. You know — we've got to hurry up — and afterwards I've
got to be in his office in thirty minutes! And you have to drive me
there because he doesn't want me to exert myself —
(*She hurries to door right*)

AUGIE

Baby, can't we put it off until tomorrow?

ISOLDE

No, we can't. Tomorrow won't be the same.

AUGIE

Tonight?

ISOLDE

(*Crossing back to center*)
He won't be in his office tonight. He's waiting for us *now!* If
you're too tired to drive me, I can call a cab.

AUGIE

(*Pathetically*)
That's not the point.
(*Sits up*)
I'm perfectly willing to *drive* you —

ISOLDE

Well, what is it, then?

31

AUGIE

(*Half-reclining again*)

Look, darling, I've been in town since this morning. It was a hundred and five — people were dropping like flies. I left my footprints in the cement — all I want to do is take a cold shower and get into —

(*Switches quickly*)

All I want to do is take a cold shower.

ISOLDE

Augie, we're wasting valuable time. Dr. Vancouver will be leaving on the stroke of six.

AUGIE

(*Rising and getting angry*)

What does Vancouver think I am — *Univac?*

ISOLDE

I don't understand you, Augie. I thought you wanted a child as much as I do. You were willing to do anything . . .

AUGIE

I am — anything within reason.

ISOLDE

Dr. Vancouver told me, "When the graph hits this spot, get hold of your husband, and afterwards be in my office within thirty minutes!"

AUGIE

Just like that. "Here's a prescription — hurry up — fill it — I'm double-parked."

32

ISOLDE

(*Annoyed*)

Are you or are you *not* going to cooperate?

AUGIE

(*Wistfully, crossing to* ISOLDE)

Honey, I *want* to cooperate — believe me — but you've got to take *my* graph into consideration. You've got to give me a little time.

ISOLDE

(*Breaks in*)

We haven't *got* any time. It's got to be *now*.

AUGIE

(*Pleadingly*)

Isolde —

ISOLDE

(*Icily, backing two steps*)

What?

AUGIE

Darling, believe me — I love you — and I want to do anything in the world to make you happy. But I can't meet a deadline.

(ISOLDE *glares at him and crosses to phone. She dials five numerals*)

ISOLDE

Hello. Dr. Vancouver, this is Mrs. Poole. I'm terribly sorry but I couldn't get hold of my husband, so I don't think you'd better

33

wait. Yes, I'm sorry too, Doctor, but I'm afraid it can't be helped. But thanks for trying, Doctor. Good-by.

(*She hangs up and starts back into house. He steps in front of her*)

AUGIE

Isolde, forgave me — it isn't my fault. It's atavistic — something deep down in my nature says the night was made for love . . .

ISOLDE

Oh, save those captions for your cartoons!

(*She crosses below him and exits. He looks after her, crosses to sit in swivel chair, thinks a moment, presses two phone buttons*)

AUGIE

Isolde? Isolde?

ISOLDE'S VOICE

(*Off stage, through the mike*)

What?

AUGIE

Darling, I'm sorry — but you know I want a child just as much as you do — maybe even more. You know that, don't you?

ISOLDE'S VOICE

You always said you did —

AUGIE

And you know how much I adore you —

34

THE TUNNEL OF LOVE

ISOLDE'S VOICE

There are times when I ask myself, is love enough?

AUGIE

(*Rises*)

That's a fair question — and I don't know the answer. I'm a weak character, that's true — but I warned you about that before we were married. And I'm a failure to boot — but I told you at the time I was a potential failure.

(*He is facing left, so he does not see her enter*)

My one redeeming feature is that I've never wavered in my love for you.

(ISOLDE *stands leaning against door. She has changed to a fetching blue robe*)

But maybe you're right — maybe love is *not* enough.

ISOLDE

Oh, you contemptible cad!

AUGIE

(*Turns and beams*)

Darling!

(*He hurries toward her. She meets him and they embrace*)

ISOLDE

How can I keep falling for that poor helpless boy routine?

AUGIE

Thank God you do!

35

ISOLDE

And promise me you'll never use that word failure again — even kidding!

AUGIE

I promise! Let's drink on it.
                    (*Crosses to bar*)
Suddenly I'm parched.

ISOLDE

        (*Follows him, sees champagne for first time*)
Where did *that* come from?

AUGIE

The Peppers.

                    (*Lifts out bottle*)
Piper Heidsieck! The Miller's High Life of champagnes.

ISOLDE

Aren't they sweet? They've been so darling and thoughtful.

AUGIE

        (*Pouring two glasses of champagne*)
Yes, there are credits and debits having your best friends living across the road.
            (*He gives her glass and raises his*)
To you, my fairest love —

ISOLDE

And to you, my darling —
            (*They drink, then she sits on sofa*)

36

Oh, Augie, I must have scared hell out of you. Probably gave you a trauma.

AUGIE

(*He sits beside her, placing bottle on floor beside him*)
It *was* a little unexpected.

ISOLDE

I'll never do that to you again. From now on we'll let nature carry the ball.

AUGIE

And from now on let *me* call the signals.

ISOLDE

I'm sure that Rock-a-bye will have one for us eventually.

AUGIE

Of course they will. The main thing is, we *want* a child. And if we want one enough, somehow, somewhere we'll get one. So let's just relax and see what happens.

ISOLDE

(*Stroking his head, which is on her shoulder*)
Oh, my Augie — my poor little fellow.

AUGIE

(*Smiles*)
And when we *do* get a baby, you can stop mothering me so much.
(*He picks up bottle*)

ISOLDE

Am I mothering you? I didn't realize —

37

AUGIE

I like it, but it's not good for me.
(*Pours into his glass*)
Saps the little male insolence I was born with.

ISOLDE

You have plenty of male insolence — don't give me that.

AUGIE

(*Sets down bottle and drinks*)
Oh, Dick opened that can of tomatoes again about selling my ideas . . .

ISOLDE

You didn't accept?

AUGIE

No, but maybe I should. We can't keep living on your grandmother's money. Not that I'm too honorable, but it's running out. Anyway, I'm no artist — I'm a gag man, and I may as well settle for that.

ISOLDE

Never! Never to my dying day will I let you settle for anything less than you want to be.

AUGIE

If Van Gogh had married a woman like you, he'd still have both his ears.

ISOLDE

Maybe we made a mistake — buying this house. We managed on a lot less down on Barrow Street.

AUGIE

We had to — we *had* a lot less. But when we have kids, you'll be glad we're out here. The city's no place to bring up children.

ISOLDE

I suppose you're right. But I loved our first year in the Village . . .

AUGIE

You know what I remember most vividly about those days? Those long winter afternoons without any heat, when we had to get into bed to keep warm.

(*They kiss. He crosses to phone, starts to dial. On fourth numeral —*)

CURTAIN FALLS

Scene Two

TIME: *The next day.*

AT RISE: *We find* AUGIE *seated at his drawing board, sketching. The outside door is open. Suddenly he spots a mouse creeping along the floor, next to the opposite wall. He rises stealthily, watching its progress, and fires his slipper across the room. The mouse disappears into a hole under the fireplace.*

AUGIE
(Crossing, he picks up slipper and puts it on)
Damn mice! Barns! Everybody knows this barn is converted but the mice. I wish I were back in the Village where the rats come out and fight.

(He gets out a pair of bicycle clips from bottom of phone stand and, resting his foot on champagne drum, puts one around his pants at the ankle. As he puts on the second bicycle clip, DICK *enters.)*

DICK
(Looks at the clips on AUGIE's *trousers)*
Hi, Augie! Going bicycling?

AUGIE
No. Mice.

40

DICK

(*Goes to phone*)

Mind if I use your phone?

AUGIE

Your phone out of order?

DICK

No. I can't make this at home.

AUGIE

Oh, a personal call.

(AUGIE *crosses right, picks up darts from end of fireplace*)

I see that quivering conscience of yours has subsided.

DICK

(*Annoyed. To* AUGIE)

I'll get to you in a minute. . . .

(*Into phone*)

Westport Arms? Miss McBain, please . . . No answer? . . . No, no message. I'll call later.

(AUGIE *throws dart at target hung on door right.* DICK *hangs up, looks at* AUGIE, *crosses*)

Now. You've been taking pot shots at my morality, and I don't like it.

AUGIE

I don't care what you do on your own time, but we're trying to get a baby. And while you're my reference I wish you'd cool off. I might as well have given Rubirosa.

(*Throws second dart*)

DICK

That's just an excuse. You don't want to see anyone enjoying something you can't enjoy yourself. You'd be doing the same thing I'm doing if you weren't frightened.

AUGIE

Down, boy, down.

DICK

Oh, yes! It's the old story. Scratch a censor and you'll find a satyr.

AUGIE

A *what?*

DICK

A *scared* satyr.
(*He takes third dart from* AUGIE *and throws it*)
You're something very old in American life — the Passionate Puritan — Jonathan Edwards preaching fire and brimstone — denying to others what he fears in himself.
(AUGIE *laughs*)
Trying to laugh it off is just another defense.

AUGIE

Okay. Let's not laugh it off. Let's put it on the line.

DICK

Shoot. It'll clear the air for both of us.
(*Looks at his watch, sits on bench*)
You're on.

42

AUGIE

You, on the other hand, are something *new* in American life —
a rebel in Brooks Brothers clothes — dreaming of setting up a
middle-class Montparnasse out here in the suburbs.

DICK

(*A pained smile*)

Jargon — double-talk.

AUGIE

(*Ignores him*)

I've seen you on Sundays, sipping *espresso* while the children
are in church. Bar-car Existentialists, reading Sartre behind a
picture window — keeping your wives on the assembly line while
you're scratching for love on Madison Avenue — drinking brandy
after PTA meetings — always broke on twenty thousand a year.
You're a new American class — the Babbitt Bohemian!

DICK

(*Rises*)

Are you through?

AUGIE

Not quite —

(ISOLDE *comes in, wearing the new watermelon shantung
dress and carrying bottle of nail polish*)

ISOLDE

Here's that dress I bought yesterday. How do you like it?

DICK

(*Appreciatively*)

A knockout! Alice used to look like that — once.

43

AUGIE

And she will again if you give her a chance.

DICK

I'll live my life, you live yours — Brother Jonathan!
(*He goes, closing door*)

ISOLDE

(*Sits on sofa*)

What's that about?

AUGIE

(*Crossing*)

Nothing. Isolde, do we *have* to go over there for dinner tonight?

ISOLDE

(*Starts doing nails*)

I don't see how we can get out of it. Anyway, I thought you were such good friends.

AUGIE

We are. Only there are times when he bores me with all that tripe he spouts. A free, uninhibited soul — !
(*Takes cartoon from drawing board, sits in swivel chair and starts to draw*)

ISOLDE

Everybody in Westport's on to Dick. He hasn't fooled anybody but Alice in years. He sees himself as a dashing, romantic figure, but with each success he has to keep confirming it all over again.

AUGIE

(*Nods*)

Poor tortured soul, driven from one gorgeous dame to another.

ISOLDE

He's a fascinating case history.

AUGIE

(*Rises, puts cartoon on drawing board*)

I never realized you were so tolerant.

ISOLDE

(*Earnestly*)

"To know all is to forgive all."

AUGIE

Secretly you admire him. Dashing — daring — a hell of a fellow, isn't he?

ISOLDE

I used those words in a derogatory sense. But you wouldn't understand Dick. You're far too normal.

AUGIE

Normal! I wish everybody'd stop calling me normal!

(*Accusingly*)

You mean inhibited, don't you? Telling everyone at the Mullers' the other night what a simple, uncomplicated, easygoing husband I am. Why don't you build me up the way other wives build *their* husbands up?

45

ISOLDE

(*Rising*)

What do you mean, build you up?

AUGIE

Stop making me out a cheerful moron! I've got just as many blocks and neuroses, and I can be just as difficult and dashing and daring as any of those other bastards around here, and don't you forget it!

(ISOLDE *shakes her head tolerantly*)

ISOLDE

I'd love to know what happened before I came in to put you in this frame of mind.

AUGIE

Nothing happened! Nothing ever happens to me, you know that.

(*He goes toward bathroom door*)

Plod, plod, plod!

(*He turns*)

And stop being so damned tolerant! Nothing is more irritating than that!

(*He goes off into bathroom.* ISOLDE *hesitates, puzzled, then starts right as* ALICE *enters outside door and stops her. She's excited*)

ALICE

Isolde! She's *here!*

ISOLDE

Who is?

ALICE

(*They sit on bench*)

It's the oddest thing. When I got home there was a strange car parked in the driveway, and this woman sitting on the porch, waiting for me.

ISOLDE

Who? What woman?

ALICE

From Rock-a-bye. The investigator. Her name is Estelle Novick.

ISOLDE

(*A quick look at bathroom*)

Oh, God!

ALICE

She's *very* businesslike and shrewd, but I gave you a terrific send-off. Just hope I didn't lay it on too thick.

ISOLDE

(*Nervously*)

Thanks. Where is she now?

ALICE

She just went over to the Marshalls' to check up on *them.*

ISOLDE

What for?

ALICE

They always keep tabs on adopted parents for the first year —
until the baby is legal.

ISOLDE
(*Rises*)

Oh . . . Of all the days!

ALICE

Why?

ISOLDE

Augie's in a foul mood. He did his best to pick a fight with me,
but I wouldn't let him.

ALICE

What's wrong?

ISOLDE

Oh, I don't know. He's depressed about his work — money —
and other things. I think he's developing a deep sense of inade-
quacy, and he's compensating by lashing out at *me*.

ALICE

Oh, Isolde, you're wonderful! I wish I'd taken psychology when
I was in college.
(*Remembering*)
Listen — she'll be here any minute.
(*She looks at bar, starts toward it*)
You'd better change. You look too darned sophisticated. Slip
into something sweet and motherly.

(*She takes gin and Scotch bottles off bar and hides them on floor below*)

Have you got a dirndl?

(ISOLDE *nods and starts right.* ALICE *follows*)

Well, put it on. And take off those earrings and comb your hair down — and nice flat shoes —

ISOLDE

I know what I'll do! I'm a Brownie leader. I'll put on my Scout uniform!

(*They exit into house as bathroom door flies open and* AUGIE *comes out in white shirt, blue undershorts, and barefoot sandals. He is chasing mouse, slapping at floor with a bath towel*)

AUGIE

Now you're going too far! Taking advantage, you little rat.

(*Mouse darts down right and disappears under fireplace*)

Hide in my bathroom, will you? Come here, dammit!

(*He glares after mouse, frustrated, then turns and starts back into bathroom*)

Lousy mice all over the joint. Wait'll I get that exterminator.

(*Crosses down to bar*)

Who's been fooling around this bar? Where the hell — ?

(*He lifts lid, looks inside, lets lid slam. Sees bottles hidden on floor, picks up Scotch*)

Oh, hiding, eh?

(*There's a knock on front door. He starts to answer, stops halfway to wrap towel around his middle, sarong-fashion. He opens door, still carrying bottle of Scotch, revealing* ESTELLE NOVICK, *a very lovely young woman in a tailored suit. She enters*)

NOVICK

Mr. Poole?

AUGIE

(*Curiously*)

Uh-huh.

NOVICK

(*Takes in the Scotch with a disapproving look*)
May I come in?

AUGIE

(*Wonderingly*)

Yes, please do.
(*She enters further, taking in the interior.* AUGIE *is behind her, looking at her, puzzled*)

NOVICK

Is Mrs. Poole at home?

AUGIE

(*Nods*)
She's probably dressing. I'll go get her.
(*Crosses right, very dignified. Turning at door*)
Who shall I say is calling?

50

NOVICK

Estelle Novick.

(AUGIE *suddenly sees the mouse running along the floor-board upstage. He dashes to it, slapping at it with the towel*)

AUGIE

Oh, coming back for more, huh? This time you won't make it! —

A mouse. Don't worry. I'll get him!

(AUGIE *misses the mouse again as it disappears. He turns*)

Gone, dammit! He's in training and I'm not — that's the trouble. It's a mouse.

NOVICK

Mr. Poole!

AUGIE

(*Reassuringly. He sets bottle down and wraps towel around him*)

It's all right — he's gone. . . . Can I get you a drink?

NOVICK

No, thank you.

AUGIE

(*He picks up bottle*)

Won't you please sit down?

(*She looks uncertainly in direction mouse disappeared*)

Oh, he won't be back for a while — until he gets his second wind.

(*She sits on sofa.* AUGIE *holds up bottle*)

Sure you won't change your mind?

NOVICK

No, thanks.

AUGIE

(*Crossing to bar*)

Well, I think I'd better have one. I've been tense all day.

NOVICK

(*Interestedly*)

What do you attribute your tension to, Mr. Poole?

AUGIE

(*Shrugs as he pours*)

Probably these damn mice. We can't lick 'em. . . . Well, if we can't lick 'em, maybe we ought to join 'em.

(*Drinks, pleased with his own humor*)

I'll go get my wife.

(*He crosses right*)

You and Isolde old pals from Bennington? Every once in a while some girl drops in and she's an old pal from Bennington. You sound like the Bennington type.

NOVICK

No, I went to the Sorbonne.

AUGIE

(*Turns back*)

Sorbonne, huh?

NOVICK

At present I am an exchange student at Columbia. I am doing social work while I am writing my doctor's thesis.

AUGIE

Why can't your doctor write his own thesis?
(*He shakes with laughter*)
I've had that gag bottled up for ten years, waiting for someone to say what you just said. That calls for a drink.
(*He drinks*)
Come on, let me fix you one.

NOVICK

(*She places purse and gloves on coffee table*)
No, thanks. I never drink while I'm on duty.
(*As she straightens up he sees red feather on her lapel and indicates it*)

AUGIE

Oh, Community Chest, huh?

NOVICK

I give what I can.

AUGIE

Well, it's a very worthy cause. I'll make a contribution. We may be using it ourselves any day now.
(*He lifts his glass*)

If the price of Scotch keeps going up. Sure you won't have one?
(*She shakes her head.* AUGIE *crosses to bar*)
Well, I think I'd better have another.
(*He pours another drink*)

NOVICK

I find most people drink to escape from something. What do *you* drink to escape from, Mr. Poole?

AUGIE

The ravages of alcohol.
(*He drinks*)

NOVICK

Very amusing. What school did *you* go to, Mr. Poole?

AUGIE

I never went past high school.

NOVICK

How did you get along there?

AUGIE

Terrible. Everybody hated me because I was so popular.
(*She looks bored. He shrugs, raises eyebrows, and crosses to sofa*)
Tell me, Miss Novick, what's this thesis you're writing about?

54

NOVICK

I am doing research on "The Paradox of Sex in New England Culture."

AUGIE

Wow! You should have a great time, researching sex in Westport.

NOVICK

It's difficult doing it alone.

AUGIE

(*Nodding*)

Practically impossible.

NOVICK

There should be a whole team to cover a cross section of the field. Tell me, Mr. Poole, do you like children?

AUGIE

Crazy about 'em.

(*Sits on sofa*)

As a matter of fact, I'm trying to adopt one.

NOVICK

That's commendable. Do you realize what you're letting yourself in for?

AUGIE

I sure do. And you can bet on one thing — none of that progressive crap around here!

NOVICK

I see you have theories, Mr. Poole.

AUGIE

I certainly have!

NOVICK

How would you deal with a child who won't eat?

AUGIE

Send him to bed without any supper.

NOVICK

And how would you compare the problem of raising children from one to five, with those from five to seven? Which do you think is the more important period?

AUGIE

(*He thinks seriously for a long moment*)
Five to seven.

NOVICK

Why?

AUGIE

Because that's the cocktail hour.
(*He shakes with laughter.* DICK *comes in from outside, cheerfully. He's wearing a smart pair of walking shorts and sport shirt. He stops and stares as he sees them. Finally, he goes back to door and knocks*)

AUGIE

It's all right. You can come in.
(*He rises*)

DICK

(*Smiles knowingly as he crosses down*)
I can? Thanks. . . . Thought it might be private.
(*He looks* AUGIE *over in amusement.* AUGIE *becomes aware of his undress*)

AUGIE

Oh!
(*Flustered*)
I was just dressing —
(*He starts to bathroom*)
This is Miss Novick — Community Chest . . . Mr. Pepper. Be right back, Miss Novick.
(*He's off.* DICK *smiles at* NOVICK *and crosses to her, immediately on the prowl. She rises*)

DICK

(*Jovially*)
Well, well! Nice to know you, Miss Novick.
(*They shake hands*)
The Community Chest is looking up. I guess you were about to call on me. I live right across the road.
(*He takes a card from his wallet*)
Look, honey, I take care of all my charities at the office. Drop in and see me any day around one. We can have lunch together and discuss the whole situation.

57

NOVICK

(*Taking card coolly, crosses to bench*)
What situation?

DICK

(*Following her, smiling*)
Anything — community problems — our own problems — you
name it.

(*Puts wallet back in pocket*)

NOVICK

Aren't you married, Mr. Pepper?

DICK

Sure. Aren't you?

NOVICK

No.

(*She returns his card*)
How would your wife feel about your making dates like this?

DICK

Would you like me to bring a note from her saying it's okay?
Now, what's a good day? If you can't come to see me, I'll break
down and go to see you.

(AUGIE *comes in from bathroom with slacks on, tying his
tie, still in sandals*)

AUGIE

If you just wait a second, I'll get my checkbook —

NOVICK

(*Crossing to coffee table for gloves and purse*)
Don't bother, Mr. Poole.

AUGIE

(*Crosses to sofa*)

Why not?

NOVICK

And I think you ought to know that your friend made a pass
at me.

AUGIE

(*Laughs*)
Naturally — but is that any reason you can't accept my dona-
tion?

DICK

(*Indignantly*)
Pass? You call *that* a pass?

NOVICK

Mr. Pepper, perhaps I'd better tell you who I am. I'm from
Rock-a-bye.

AUGIE

Rock-a-bye? Why that's the agency — we're trying to —
(*As it sinks in, he slumps down on arm of sofa*)
— obtain — a — baby from . . .

NOVICK

Yes, that's why I'm here.

59

AUGIE

(*Stares open-mouthed*)
You mean you're the — *investigator?*

NOVICK

I am — unfortunately.

DICK

(*Outraged*)
Well! Of all the lousy tricks! Telling me you were from the Community Chest!

NOVICK

(*Mildly*)
I did *not*. Mr. Poole told you.

AUGIE

(*Rising*)
Sure I told him, but that's beside the point! If you're going to be an investigator, *look* like one! That aphrodisiac perfume you've got on, and that subversive neckline . . . What the hell is this — an obstacle course?

NOVICK

You're being absurd. You can't excuse his behavior by switching to an attack on me. *I'm* not under scrutiny.

DICK

You are in my book! You and your whole Beddie-Bye. Your superiors will hear about this, my good woman!

AUGIE

(*To* DICK, *angrily*)
Will you please shut up, and stop making threats!

60

NOVICK

I'm sorry, Mr. Poole, but I have to enter the fact in my report — your reference made a pass at me.

DICK

Stop calling it a pass. It was a charming invitation to lunch.

AUGIE

(*To* NOVICK)
What's that got to do with *me*? Am I my brother's keeper?

NOVICK

I'm sorry, Mr. Poole. It isn't just your reference. I'm afraid that you're not ideal father material.

AUGIE

And I suppose he *is!*
(*Indicating* DICK)
Just because he's a do-it-yourself addict.
(*Pleadingly*)
Now wait, Miss Novick — please don't make any snap judgments. You don't know how much this means to us. I'll get another reference. He was my wife's idea. I'm a very loyal and devoted husband. Don't go by him. Why, I'm the laughingstock of Westport, I'm so inhibited!

NOVICK

You are?

AUGIE

Just sexually. Otherwise I'm warm and affectionate and outgoing. Everything a father *should* be.

61

NOVICK

Mr. Poole, you must realize that we have a great responsibility to those little lives. What I have to decide is whether I might be placing a child in a home that may be broken. Do you ever think of the victims of broken homes?

AUGIE

Yes. And when I can no longer bear to think of them, I think of the victims of intact ones. I know parents right this minute you should be out taking children away from!
(*He shoots a look at* DICK)

NOVICK

(*Shrugs, crossing center*)
I am sorry but that is not my job. Good day, Mr. Poole.

DICK

(*Stopping her*)
Can't you be a little human? I made a mistake, but that's the way I am — disarmingly direct, playful, even childlike —

NOVICK

Unfortunately, Mr. Pepper, we're not putting *you* out for adoption.
(*She goes to door*)
Good day, gentlemen.
(ISOLDE *and* ALICE *come in from house.* ISOLDE *is wearing* Scout uniform)

ALICE

Oh, there you are, Miss Novick. This is Mrs. Poole.
(ISOLDE *crosses to* NOVICK)

62

NOVICK

(*Hand on the door*)

How do you do, Mrs. Poole.

ISOLDE

You're not *leaving*, are you?

NOVICK

Yes, I am. Mr. Poole and Mr. Pepper told me everything I need to know.

ISOLDE

(*Bewildered*)

Don't you want to interview me? I'm going to be the mother.

NOVICK

(*A little smile*)

It really won't be necessary. Thank you so much. Good-by.

(*She goes out. The girls exchange bewildered looks*)

ISOLDE

(*Coming center*)

That's the oddest thing —

ALICE

What could have happened? *Something* must have happened.

AUGIE

(*Crossing to* ISOLDE)

Nothing happened. I was chasing a mouse and she busted in.

63

ISOLDE

(*Gets a whiff of him*)

And you were *drinking* too!

AUGIE

(*Defiantly*)

I had a drink, yes! What about it?

ISOLDE

(*Looks at* AUGIE *miserably*)

Oh, Augie — what *else?*

AUGIE

Frankly, I am very unimpressed with Rock-a-bye. It can't be much if that's a sample of their stuff. I think we ought to forget them and apply to some other place.

ALICE

Why, Rock-a-bye has one of the best reputations in the East! They get some of the best babies there. They're right between Yale and Smith!

ISOLDE

(*Almost weeping*)

Augie, we're not supposed to pass on *them* — they're passing on *us!* What did she *say?* Did she say we'd *hear* from them?

AUGIE

She said she'd definitely make a report.

ISOLDE

I know exactly what happened! You made a fool of yourself, didn't you? I can see it all — running around in your bare feet,

half drunk! No wonder the woman couldn't wait to get out of
here.

(*She turns from him*)

AUGIE
(*Very guiltily, following her*)
Now, baby, there are lots of other places. There's the Cradle,
the Crib —

ISOLDE
(*Taking off beret*)
After all we've gone through to get this far!

AUGIE
Isolde, darling, listen —

ISOLDE
(*Pushes him away and crosses to* ALICE)
Oh, leave me alone!

ALICE
Come on, darling, come over to my place.
(*She leads* ISOLDE *to door, looking over at* AUGIE *and
motioning that it'll be all right later*)

ISOLDE
And to think I put on this uniform.
(*They exit.* DICK *starts to door.* AUGIE *shoots him a look*)

DICK
(*Very guiltily*)
Augie — I'm terribly sorry.
(*Crossing to sofa*)

65

But did I know who she was? You told me Community Chest —
and I figured it was time I got something out of *them.*

AUGIE

Are you out for a world's record? Can't you pass up *one dame?*

DICK

(*Virtuously*)

I have never yet gone after a woman unless she sent out a
certain signal — like radar.

AUGIE

I didn't notice any signal.

DICK

Of course not. Your sensory perceptions have been blunted by
years of disuse. She lit up like that sign on the Garden —
"Wrestling Tonight." I'm not what she's looking for — but she's
looking. Mark my words.

AUGIE

(*Bitterly*)

My friend — my reference. . . . What are you trying to prove?

DICK

(*Nods and sits heavily on sofa*)

You're right. What *am* I trying to prove? I've asked myself the
same question a hundred times. And every time an affair is over
I have a terrific sense of guilt.

AUGIE

But you wait till it's over.

DICK

Yes. I feel I deserve this guilt, and when I don't have it I'm uncomfortable and I try to recapture the guilt by sleeping around.

AUGIE

Why the hell do you sleep around then, if it's that much trouble?

DICK

My masochistic urge — my need to suffer. It's the only way of getting back to the guilt.

AUGIE

Oh, you've got to get back to it, huh?

DICK

Yes. I have it coming to me for sleeping around. That's why I'm going to an analyst.

AUGIE

Does he tell you all this?

DICK

No, *I* tell *him*. You don't know what I'm going through. How could you?

AUGIE

Of course. How could I? I'm too damn normal!

DICK

Normal?! You're all tied up in knots. That's why you don't have any children.

AUGIE

That's ridiculous! That might be true of a woman —

DICK

(*Breaks in scornfully, rising*)
If *you're* tied up in knots, don't you think it communicates itself
to your wife?
(*Crossing to* AUGIE)
Why, that's elementary. Don't argue with me — I know all
about it. I owe the man twenty-five hundred dollars.

AUGIE

He must be a brilliant guy to let you get into him for that much.

DICK

That's not the point. The point is you won't get anywhere until
you unwind. And you won't unwind until you break out of your
cocoon. Live a little — it's not going to hurt Isolde, it'll *help* her.
It'll help you both.

AUGIE

(*Arm on* DICK's *shoulder*)
According to your logic, if I have an affair with another woman,
I'll have a child with my own wife?

DICK

I don't guarantee it. But what can you lose? You're not getting
anywhere *your* way.

AUGIE

(*Turns him, takes his elbow, and leads him to door, grimly*)
Thank you, Doctor, I can't tell you how much better I feel.
(*He shoves* DICK *out door, slamming it behind him*)

Insufferable ass! Trying to get me to join his Share-the-Guilt Club. *He* talks about paranoiacs — the blind-to-yourself department.

(*He picks up cartoon from drawing board, takes out cigarette, crosses to phone, presses button and dials five numbers. He crosses to coffee table for matches as —*)

ALICE'S VOICE

Hello?

AUGIE

Alice, is Isolde there?

(*Lights cigarette*)

ALICE'S VOICE

Oh, Augie, hurry up. We're waiting for you.

AUGIE

Put Isolde on, will you please?

ALICE'S VOICE

Isolde, it's Augie —

ISOLDE'S VOICE

(*Off*)

What does *he* want?

ALICE'S VOICE

What do you want?

AUGIE

Let me talk to her.

ALICE'S VOICE

He wants to talk to you.

ISOLDE

Tell him I'm busy.

ALICE'S VOICE

She says she's —

AUGIE

(*By drawing board, talking towards phone*)
I heard it! Listen, Alice, I'm not going over there to dinner —
I'm not in the mood to be with anybody. Tell her I thought we'd
go out somewhere, just the two of us.

ALICE'S VOICE

He says he wants to go out alone with you. He's not in the
mood to be with anybody.

ISOLDE'S VOICE

Why doesn't *he* go out? Because frankly, I'm not in the mood
to be with *him.*

ALICE'S VOICE

Anything else?

AUGIE

No, that's plenty.
(*He pushes button*)
It's so unfair! Guilt by association, by God! I won't crawl. The
hell with it!

70

(There's a knock on the door. He drops cartoon on coffee
table, crosses to door and opens it. NOVICK *steps in, smiling*
rather guiltily. AUGIE, *glumly*)

Oh? What are *you* doing here? Going to nail a denunciation on
my door?

NOVICK

No . . . This is an unofficial call . . . May I come in?

AUGIE

Look, Miss Novick, if you want to play Margaret Mead, go to
Scarsdale.

NOVICK

(She steps in. He closes door, steps down to her)
Please, Mr. Poole, I've been thinking it over. It *was* partly my
fault, and if you can find another reference, we'll reconsider your
application.

AUGIE

(Excitedly)
Oh, that's wonderful, Miss Novick! I'll call my wife! She's just
across the road!
(He starts to phone)

NOVICK

Wait.
(He stops)
I made a few remarks about you as a father — and I want you
to realize there was nothing personal — just my job. Personally,
I think you're a very attractive man, Mr. Poole.

71

AUGIE

(*Delighted, he straightens shoulders*)

You do, huh? Deep down I knew *you* were warm and human, Miss Novick. Don't worry — I'll get an impeccable reference this time if I have to go to — to Bridgeport!

(*He crosses to telephone*)

NOVICK

Surely you know a nice family man in this community?

AUGIE

I know dozens. But if *you* go calling on them I can't guarantee anything!

NOVICK

(*Crossing below sofa*)

Why, thank you, Mr. Poole.

(*He starts to dial*)

I'll take that drink now.

(*He looks at her in surprise, his dialing arrested*)

I'm off duty.

(*She tosses bag and gloves on sofa*)

AUGIE

(*Behind the bar, putting ice in glass*)

Fine! A dual personality. Stern and forbidding during the work-a-day, charming and feminine after dark. What'll you have?

NOVICK

A double Scotch, please.

AUGIE

A *really* dual personality. You know something? I knew you were regular the minute you brushed off Dick Pepper.
(*Pours his own drink*)

NOVICK
(*Crosses below bar*)

Thanks. I'd rather not discuss your friend. He's much too obvious.

AUGIE
(*Delighted*)

He's just prematurely neurotic.
(*Hands her drink and leans forward confidently as she sits on bar stool*)
Can I tell you something? Secretly I've been admiring him.
(*Pours his own drink*)

NOVICK

Oh, *no!* He's a true aborigine, only he wears walking shorts instead of a loincloth.

AUGIE

Dick Pepper, the Abercrombie and Fitch aborigine!
(*Both drink*)

NOVICK

In New Guinea they know how to deal with such men.

73

AUGIE

(*Eagerly*)

They do, huh?

NOVICK

They'd drum him out of the tribe.

AUGIE

(*Laughs*)

And make him turn in his loincloth.

(*He sits on other bar stool*)

NOVICK

Last year I made a study of sex in New Guinea — I am making a study of sexual patterns around the globe.

AUGIE

(*He considers this a moment*)

Fascinating! Well, you've come to the right place for it. This community is a perfect testing ground. A self-contained suburbia — like a rare French vineyard that produces one of those amusing little wines — just a narrow strip along the sunny slope of the New Haven Railroad, in Fairfield County.

NOVICK

(*Laughs*)

Yes, this area *has* got a very special bouquet. The natives here have strange taboos.

(*She drinks, looking at him*)

AUGIE

(*He looks her over admiringly*)

It's hard to think of you as a man of science, Miss Novick.

NOVICK

I run into that all the time.

AUGIE

I'll bet!

NOVICK

Actually, in some ways my appearance is a handicap. It's hard for people to take me seriously — and I'm quite serious. It's my life. It's going to take the place of home and marriage for me. For instance, after I get my degree I hope to join a team of anthropologists and continue my studies of sex in New Zealand and the Australian Archipelago.

AUGIE

(*Nods*)

I suppose there's a lot of that going on *there,* too.
(*Both drink. He laughs delightedly, dashes behind bar*)
Have another drink, Miss Novick!
(*He pours Scotch in glasses, as she rises and removes jacket*)
You know what, Miss Novick? You make me *glad* I'm inhibited.

NOVICK

You keep saying you're inhibited, but I don't see any evidence of it.

AUGIE

(*Lies across bar*)

That's the strange thing. I feel relaxed with you — *released* — you know what I mean?

NOVICK

Yes, I think I do. It's what the poets call the shock of recognition.

(*She takes drink, crosses to sofa, sits, and crosses legs*)

AUGIE

Yeah, the shock of recognition.
(*He drinks. To himself*)
Maybe he was right.

NOVICK

Who?

AUGIE

(*Gets up and swaggers above sofa*)
You doing anything tonight?

NOVICK

Not really.

AUGIE

Neither am I.

NOVICK

What about Mrs. Poole?

AUGIE

Mrs. Poole walked out in high dudgeon and left me to my own devices.

(*Leans over back of sofa*)

76

Will you be one of my devices, Miss Novick? We'll drive into town tonight for dinner. I know a lovely spot with an air-conditioned garden. We'll put the top down and let the wind rush through our hair. . . . In the interest of pure research, Doc. I want to be on your team.

NOVICK

(*Laughs*)

I'd love it.

AUGIE

Great! I'll get dressed.
(*He takes her empty glass, looks at it in startled admiration*)
Another double while you're waiting?

NOVICK

Thanks.
(*He laughs lecherously, goes to bar and pours two drinks as she rises and picks up cartoon from coffee table. She starts to laugh*)

AUGIE

(*Delightedly*)
My dear girl! Laughing out loud at my stuff! What are you trying to do?
(*She drops cartoon on sofa*)
Overpower me?

77

(He comes over to her with the two glasses. Instead of taking hers, she puts her arms around him and kisses him, as he holds the glasses in both hands, arms outstretched. After a moment they both slip from his nerveless fingers and crash to the floor, as —)

CURTAIN FALLS

ACT TWO

ACT TWO

Scene One

TIME: *A Sunday morning in September. Church bell rings in distance.*

AT RISE: AUGIE *peers out window anxiously, consults his watch, then crosses to phone and dials. Church bell stops ringing.*

AUGIE

Hello? Dick? . . . Can you come over here right away? I've got something to talk to you about. . . . Well, as soon as you're dressed. It's kind of important.

(*He hangs up. There is a tremendous thump at outside door. He crosses and opens door. A huge pile of Sunday papers is on the mat. He calls off angrily*)

It's a good thing you didn't hit the house! You'd have knocked it over.

(*Bicycle bell sounds an impudent reply.* ISOLDE *comes in from the house as he bends over and lifts the papers with a grunt. She carries a tray with coffeepot and two cups, crosses to coffee table*)

ISOLDE

Sunday papers come?

AUGIE

Uh-huh. Sunday papers!
(*He struggles to sofa with them*)
No wonder this country is full of slipped discs.
(*Silently, he extracts magazine section and hands it to her. She pours his coffee and hands it to him. She sits on sofa, as he settles on bench with coffee and real estate section*)

AUGIE

Now — what's new in the real estate section?

ISOLDE

You still looking? We haven't paid the interest on the mortgage for this one yet.

AUGIE

Just curious. I like to see who stuck who with what.
(*She drinks, then stretches out on sofa*)
Hey! Listen to this.
(*He reads*)
"Westport. Beautiful old colonial manse recently renovated, with lovely gristmill and pond situated behind house in sun-drenched sylvan glen." That must be Bill Johnson's dump with the swamp in back.

ISOLDE

(*Sitting up*)
You know why they're selling, don't you?

AUGIE

No. Why?

ISOLDE

They're getting a divorce.

AUGIE

(*Surprised*)

Those two? Why, they were the happiest couple west of the tollgate.

ISOLDE

She caught him — red-handed — and with her best friend.

AUGIE

(*Righteously*)

Someone she knew? That's unforgivable.

ISOLDE

(*Nods, lies back and resumes reading*)

Yes, that was her attitude.

AUGIE

I always thought Ethel was a broad-minded and understanding type —

(*Hopefully*)

— like you.

ISOLDE

(*Busy reading*)

Just thank goodness you're not Bill's type.

83

AUGIE

(*Dubiously*)

Yeah.

(*He gives her a quizzical look, but she is buried behind the paper. He goes back to his reading*)

ISOLDE

(*Excitedly, sitting up again*)

Oh, look! Here's a piece on adoption.

AUGIE

(*Looks up nervously*)

Oh?

ISOLDE

(*Reads*)

"Can the official adoption agencies meet the needs of hopeful parents?" I'd like to write an article. Bureaucrats. Red tape. It's been three months since we put in at Rock-a-bye and we haven't even heard from them — or the Cradle — or the Crib.

AUGIE

We will — I'm sure we will.

(*She lies down again and reads. After a moment, he laughs*)

Say, here's a laugh! They're putting in a new turnpike right through the Westchester Country Club, and the members are having a mass meeting to protest. Antediluvian stiffs — trying to stop progress!

(*Slight pause, then angrily*)

Hey! It's coming all the way up here. What the hell they tryin' to do — ruin Westport?

ISOLDE

Please — I'm reading.

(Pause)

Oh!

(She sits up, reading aloud)

"The adoption agencies have been subjected to criticism by unthinking hopeful parents who do not realize the difficulties of the problem."

(Picks up tray, crosses behind bench)

I'm going to write the *Times* a letter right now. Their difficulties, huh? I'll tell them a few!

AUGIE

(Alarmed)

Now, honey, don't start writing letters.

(He puts his cup on the tray)

You want to get blacklisted by every adoption agency in the country?

ISOLDE

Yes — you're right. I know! I'll sign Alice's name. She doesn't need them.

(She goes into house. AUGIE looks at his watch, goes to window, looks out, sees DICK coming, goes to door and opens it)

DICK

Hi, Augie!

85

(*He shoots past* AUGIE *to bar and starts to pour himself a drink*)
Oh — can I make you one?

AUGIE

Well, as long as it's on the house — yes.
(*Crosses and sits, on far stool*)

DICK

(*Still fixing two drinks*)
Alice hates to see me drinking in front of the kids. You wanted to see me? What is it? Oh, oh — you're worried about something — I can tell. Your jaw is slack, your eyes are glazed — you have a permanently surprised expression.

AUGIE

Odd. That describes exactly the way I feel.

DICK

What is it? You and Isolde?

AUGIE

Nope — not yet.
(DICK *drinks and crosses to sofa*)
You hear about the Johnsons selling their house and splitting up?

DICK

Yeah — Bill got caught flat-footed with a blonde viking from Darien. I had a little whirl with her myself once — just briefly — during the small-boat season.
(*He sits on sofa*)

AUGIE

So you finally worked your way down to Darien, huh?

DICK

Is that what you called me over here for? You'll drive me back to the kids.

(*He starts to rise*)

AUGIE

Dick! Wait!

(DICK *settles back*)

I'm in a jam — a bad one. I feel suffocated — as if I were drowning. Remember the evening Isolde walked out on me and I disappeared and didn't show till the next afternoon?

DICK

(*Nods*)

Yes. That was it, huh? I often wondered what you told Isolde.

AUGIE

Well, I told her I was sore at the world — got in the car — and started to drive — to cool off —

DICK

Yes?

AUGIE

Suddenly, without realizing it, I found myself in the Bronx —

DICK

(*Nods*)

So far you've sold *me*.

87

AUGIE

I said I was going over that bridge that swings open — to let the boats through — you know —

(*He demonstrates with his right arm*)

Well, when I got in the middle, it swung around — and I was on it. The machinery got stuck, and they couldn't get it back —

DICK

You're beginning to lose me.

AUGIE

(*Ignores this*)

I told her I had to sleep in the car all night till they swung it *back* again.

(*He demonstrates again*)

DICK

And she believed *that?*

AUGIE

Certainly! Why shouldn't she? I've never lied to her — before.

DICK

Amazing. And what really *did* happen?

AUGIE

(*Confidentially*)

I went down the Henry Hudson Parkway — no bridge — with a girl.

DICK
(*Rising*)

Who? Do I know her?

AUGIE

You've met her.

DICK

Yes? Yes? *Who?* Stop being coy! Spill it!

AUGIE

Miss Novick.

DICK
(*Stares*)

Who?

AUGIE

Don't you remember? The investigator from Rock-a-bye.

DICK
(*Jaw drops*)

The *dish?* No!

AUGIE
(*Nods*)

Yes. A happy choice, don't you think? I took your advice and
unwound — all around Miss Novick.

DICK

Oh, *no!* What a fool I am! I didn't expect you to take me
literally. I said what I said in self-defense — I never dreamed
you'd *act* on it.

AUGIE

(*Coldly*)

Just *why* didn't you dream I'd ever act on it?

DICK

(*Patronizingly*)

Oh, my poor boy, that sort of thing is not for you. It's out of character. You're not the type. Not with stuff like Novick. She's not for amateurs, she's for the pros!

(*He starts to laugh*)

I'm sorry, Augie — forgive me. I'm not laughing at you — it's the idea that's funny.

AUGIE

(*Blows*)

Don't you patronize me, you Madison Avenue extrovert!

DICK

(*Confidentially*)

Okay, okay . . . How long has it been going on?

AUGIE

It hasn't been going on at all. I only saw her that once — until about a week ago. She called me — said she wanted to see me — so I hightailed it up to New Haven and asked her what it was all about.

DICK

And?

AUGIE

(*Slowly*)

There was a pregnant pause.

(*There is one here.* DICK *goes to bar and pours himself a drink.* AUGIE *holds out his glass and he pours a dollop into it. They both drink*)

DICK

How far — ?

AUGIE

If winter comes, can spring be far behind?
(AUGIE *holds up three fingers.* DICK *shakes his head*)
You might at least try to buck me up — tell me it's a false alarm.

DICK

Well, I don't know. It could be. The whole thing has a sort of ghastly symmetry to it.

AUGIE

Where's my Bible?
(*He crosses to book shelves on a sudden inspiration and gets Bible*)

DICK

A little late for that, isn't it?

AUGIE

(*Sits on sofa with Bible on his knees*)
When I was a kid I had a superstition I could always get a clue to how something was going to turn out by putting my finger at random on a Bible text.

91

DICK

That's because anything can be interpreted any way that's convenient.

(AUGIE *opens Bible and brings his forefinger down on text without looking. Then he looks down and reads. A horrified expression comes over his face*)

What does it say?

AUGIE

(*Reads*)

"And Zorobabel begat Abiud and Abiud begat Eliakim and Eliakim begat Azor" — and so on for a whole chapter!

DICK

(*Crosses to sofa*)

Well, there doesn't seem to be any ambiguity about *that*.

AUGIE

Maybe I'll try two out of three.

DICK

No, that's it.

(*He closes Bible, catching* AUGIE's *finger, then places Bible on coffee table*)

What we've got to do is assume the worst and get ready for it.

AUGIE

I don't know what I'd do without you. You're so brave in the teeth of my adversity.

DICK

The first question that comes to mind is, will she lay it at your door?

AUGIE

For an editor, and a man who's supposed to know good English, *that* was certainly an ill-chosen metaphor.

DICK

What I meant was, what will she expect of you? Or what *would* she expect of you — if we can still speak in the subjunctive after all those "begats."

AUGIE

I'll do right by her. Obviously, there's only one way I can — with money.
(*He rises*)
So if the *Townsman* still wants me I'll sign that contract.

DICK
(*Unhappily*)
Sure we want you —

AUGIE

Do I get an advance if I sign?

DICK
(*Torn*)
A thousand dollars, but —

AUGIE

This is what you've been after me for — go ahead!

93

DICK

Not this way! Even an editor has his code. Anyway, this could happen to me some day — God forbid. We'll scrape up the money somehow . . . I can let you have a couple of hundred without arousing suspicion, and we'll borrow the rest, and co-sign for one another.

AUGIE

It's hopeless. Why don't I sign the contract and let's get it over?

DICK

(*Sadly*)

Okay.

AUGIE

And I've got to have the check today.

DICK

Why today?

AUGIE

I'm meeting her at one o'clock.

DICK

(*In alarm*)

Here — in Westport? You're crazy!

AUGIE

(*Nervously*)

It's my last chance. She's leaving her job and going upstate to have the baby. Look, can't you give me your personal check and collect from the office?

DICK

Okay.

(*He shakes his head patronizingly*)
You're not the cad you thought you were. Got a blank check?

AUGIE

On every bank in town.
(DICK *sits on sofa and puts on horn-rimmed glasses as*
AUGIE *gets check and pen and gives them to* DICK)
Here —
(*As* DICK *writes,* AUGIE *puts on coat and adjusts tie*)

DICK

(*Shakes his head*)
Impossible —! Where did you — ? How did you — ?
(*He stops, looks at* AUGIE *and starts to laugh*)
No! *Impossible!*

AUGIE

(*Angrily, adjusting tie*)
What the hell's so impossible about it? You're not going to
start *that* again?

DICK

I'm sorry. . . . Here . . .
(*Rises and hands check and pen to* AUGIE)

AUGIE

Thanks.

(*He indicates cartoons on drawing board*)
Take your pick — I'll see you later —
(*Starts out*)

DICK

Where are you going?

AUGIE

Church.

DICK
(*Stares*)

Church?

AUGIE
(*Nods*)
There are no atheists in foxholes. I'm meeting her there in the parking lot.

DICK

Are you out of your mind?

AUGIE

That's the safest place in town. Nobody *we* know will be there, and it's the quietest place to talk.
(*He starts to open door as* ALICE *and* ISOLDE *come in from the house, right.* ISOLDE *carries a beautiful layer cake on a plate.* DICK *crosses to above bar, taking off glasses, and picks up his drink*)

ISOLDE

Look at this beauty Alice just baked. Who'd like a slice?
(ALICE *sits gingerly on bench*)

AUGIE

It's a little early for me.
(ISOLDE *places cake on table*)

ALICE

(*Nods to* DICK's *drink*)
It's a little early for that too, isn't it? How do you think it looks when the children see their father with a highball in the middle of the day?

DICK

How do you think I could stand them if I didn't drink in the middle of the day?

AUGIE

(*Nervously, crosses to coffee table and picks up his drink*)
Anyway, we're celebrating.

ISOLDE

What?

AUGIE

I just signed a contract with the *Townsman.*

ISOLDE

(*Crosses to him*)
Darling, that's wonderful! They're using your drawings!

97

AUGIE

Well, not really my drawings. Just the gags under them.

ISOLDE

(*Unhappily*)

Oh, Augie! Why did you do it?

AUGIE

(*Nobly*)

If we're going to have a family, I've got to start making some money. My kid's got to have the best.

ISOLDE

(*Touched*)

But darling, why don't you wait till we're sure we're getting one? We're not even close.

AUGIE

Well, I want to be ready when it does happen.

ISOLDE

(*Taking* AUGIE'S *arm*)

Isn't he wonderful? How many husbands would sacrifice their careers for their home life?

AUGIE

(*Breaks in, embarrased*)

Watch it, baby —

(*Sets drink on coffee table and goes to door center*)

You're boring us. . . . I think maybe I'll go out for a little while.

ISOLDE

Where?

AUGIE

I think I'll go over to the driving range and hit a bucket of balls.
(*He exits nonchalantly with a little wave, closing door*)

ISOLDE

That's odd. He's been acting strangely for months.

ALICE
(*Eagerly*)

In what way, darling?

ISOLDE

For one thing, he's never been so thoughtful and attentive. I think I know what it is, but it's so unreasonable.
(*DICK starts mixing another drink above bar*)
Even though Dr. Vancouver has assured him, time and time again, that it's not *his* fault we haven't had a child, I'm sure that he thinks he's to blame — that there's something the matter with *him* —
(*DICK sprays soda on the bar, missing the glass*)

DICK

Oops! Sorry —
(*Takes towel from behind bar and mops up the water*)

ISOLDE

I wish you'd talk to him, Dick. Tell him it's all in his mind.

DICK

Oh, I will. I'll try to convince him it's all in his mind.
(*There's a knock at the door*)

99

ALICE

I'll get it.
(*She rises carefully, crosses and opens door, revealing*
MISS NOVICK)
Miss Novick!

NOVICK

Good afternoon, Mrs. Pepper.

ALICE

Isolde, look who's here — Miss Novick!

ISOLDE

(*Crossing up to her*)
Oh — how do you do, Miss Novick? What a surprise!

NOVICK

(*Very much at ease.* ALICE *sits on bench*)
I was just passing —

ISOLDE

(*Very flustered*)
Won't you sit down, please?
(NOVICK *crosses to sofa as* ISOLDE *closes door*)
Oh, you've met Mr. Pepper?

DICK

Yes, I've had the pleasure.
(*He sits in swivel chair.* NOVICK *sits on sofa*)

100

ISOLDE

(*Hovering over her*)

Can I get you anything? Tea? Coffee? Anything?

NOVICK

No, thanks.

ISOLDE

(*Babbling with excitement*)

I'm so glad you came back. We'd sort of given up hope of hearing from Rock-a-bye. You know we finally got rid of the mice — and my husband's on the wagon.

(*She laughs self-consciously*)

I'm so excited I don't know *what* I'm saying!

NOVICK

(*Gently*)

Mrs. Poole, perhaps I *will* have some coffee, if it isn't too much trouble.

ISOLDE

(*She turns to go*)

Not at all! Of course!

ALICE

(*Rising*)

I'll make it, dear. You stay here with Miss Novick.

ISOLDE

Thanks, dear.

(ALICE *picks up cake and hurries off right*)

Have you had lunch? How about a sandwich or something?

NOVICK

Well — maybe just a small piece of toast.

ISOLDE

Oh, yes, of course. It won't take a minute! Oh, I'm so glad you came back. My husband will be ecstatic!
(*She exits*)

DICK

(*Puts drink on bar, crosses to sofa. In hoarse whisper*)
For God's sake, why did you come *here?*

NOVICK

Really? Why not?

DICK

Please, Miss Novick — the time is past for whispering behind fans. I know all about it!

NOVICK

Oh?

DICK

Didn't you see him?

NOVICK

I must have missed him — or I had the wrong church. Where does he go?

DICK

I don't know. He never went before. He's got the check — enough to see you through. But if you need any more, get in touch with me.

NOVICK

(*Eyes him*)

That's very considerate.

DICK

(*Beginning to enjoy the role, a little pompously*)

But there's one thing I must insist on. As far as you're concerned, Augie Poole has ceased to exist.

NOVICK

(*Unruffled, rising and crossing to bench*)

I see. But what will I do about my constant reminder?

DICK

(*Uneasily, losing his grip*)

Now, look, Miss Novick, Augie's a married man. You knew that. He's in love with his wife, deeply in love. Just once his foot slipped — but he's never played around. If this happened to me I'd deserve it — but not Augie. He's too fine.

NOVICK

Please, Mr. Pepper, stop being the best friend. I have no intention of breaking up his marriage. I wouldn't hurt him for the world.

(*She sits on bench*)

Anyway, I am in transit. Next year I will be in New Zealand.

DICK

(*Crosses, shakes her hand*)

Have a wonderful trip!

NOVICK

Thank you.

DICK

I wish there were more women in the world with your principles.

NOVICK

(*Dryly*)

I'm a scientist . . . and we believe that no experience is ever wasted. Besides, it'll give me time to finish my thesis.

DICK

(*Shakes his head admiringly*)

You know — I suppose if Augie *had* to get his feet wet he couldn't have picked a better subject than you, Miss Novick!

NOVICK

Mr. Poole's a nice boy, but I wouldn't dream of marrying him even if he *were* available. As a husband he'd be impossible — otherwise he's sweet.

DICK

"Otherwise?" Who — *Augie?*

NOVICK

(*Raises her eyebrows*)

Yes. Why not?

DICK

(*Irritated*)

That's the damnedest thing I ever heard! Augie? Why, it's laughable!

(*He forces a hollow laugh*)

I *know* the boy. He's *nothing*, I tell you, strictly nothing.

104

NOVICK

Perhaps I'm in a better position to judge, Mr. Pepper.

(DICK *crosses, gets drink from bar and sits in swivel chair
as* ISOLDE *comes in with a tray containing cup of coffee and
the cake with one piece out.* ALICE *follows with piece of
cake on plate*)

ISOLDE

(*Beaming with charm*)

Here we are.

(ALICE *above bench.* ISOLDE *at end of bench*)

NOVICK

(*Rising*)

My, what an appetizing-looking cake.

ALICE

Yes. Mrs. Poole baked it this morning.

ISOLDE

(*Handing coffee to* NOVICK)

Won't you try a piece?

NOVICK

No, thanks. I must watch my figure.

ISOLDE

(*Stepping back*)

Nonsense, you have a divine figure. Hasn't she, Alice?

ALICE

(*Glumly, pulling down her anticipation blouse*)
I wish *I* had it.
(ISOLDE *places cake on table*)

NOVICK

(*As she and* ALICE *sit on bench*)
Why, Mrs. Pepper, this should be the happiest time of your life.

ALICE

It is. This time *every* year.

DICK

She's the life of the maternity ward.

ALICE

(*Eating cake*)
I'm starved!

ISOLDE

(*Crosses to sofa and sits*)
I just can't tell you how pleased I am to see you again, Miss Novick. We never did have a chance to talk.

NOVICK

I know.

ISOLDE

And Mr. Poole's been miserable because he was so sure he'd made a bad impression.

106

NOVICK

On the contrary.

(*She sips the coffee*)

ISOLDE

I suppose you'd like to know something about our education and background, Miss Novick? Well, I went to Bennington. I took a B.A.

ALICE

And she's a wonderful cook! I just *wish* you'd taste this cake.
(*She offers a bite to* NOVICK *who shakes her head*)

ISOLDE

I don't suppose a wife's reference counts for much, Miss Novick, but my husband's one of the nicest people I know. He's loyal, generous, affectionate, and unselfish.

ALICE

And I wish you could see him with our children. They adore him. He'd make a perfect father!
(*She shoots* DICK *a look*)
Wouldn't he, Dick?

DICK

Perfect.

NOVICK

Mrs. Poole, before I make my recommendation, is there anything else you'd like to tell me?

ISOLDE

Miss Novick, I may as well be frank, even if it ruins our chances. Our financial situation isn't too good. My husband's still struggling.

(*Earnestly*)

But money shouldn't be the big thing here, should it? After all, it's what we can *give* — our love, our care, our devotion — that's what really counts, isn't it?

NOVICK

(*Smiles*)

That's right, Mrs. Poole, that *is* what counts.

(*As* ISOLDE *smiles back at her in relief, the door opens and* AUGIE *comes in, looking anxious*)

DICK

(*False heartiness, rising*)

Come in, Augie. Just the usual crowd!

(AUGIE *closes door, sees* NOVICK, *stops dead*)

ISOLDE

(*She bubbles over, rising*)

Augie, darling! Miss Novick's here! She came back!

(*He tries to speak, but can't make it, and nods with a sickly smile to* NOVICK. *He comes down to* ISOLDE)

Isn't that wonderful?

ALICE

(*Gaily*)

Augie, were your ears burning?

NOVICK

(*Crosses to* AUGIE, *shakes hands, smiling charmingly*)
Hello, Mr. Poole. How nice to see you again.

ISOLDE

Miss Novick was just interviewing me. Isn't that encouraging, darling?
(AUGIE *nods.* ISOLDE *looks at* NOVICK *eagerly*)
Was there anything else you wanted to know?

NOVICK

Yes, just one thing more, Mrs. Poole. What are your feelings about the circumstances in these cases? I ask because there are some people who think these girls are "bad girls." Do you share that opinion?

ISOLDE

Oh, no! Bad girls don't get into trouble.

NOVICK

Yes — I see what you mean. Well, I really must be going. I have a long trip ahead of me.

ISOLDE

(*Going to her hopefully*)
I hope we'll see you again, Miss Novick — or hear from you?

NOVICK

Now don't raise your hopes too high, but I do know of a case. You'll have to be patient — it'll take five or six months.
(AUGIE *takes left hand out of pocket, counts on his fingers.*
He and DICK *exchange look*)

109

ISOLDE

Oh, that's nothing! If we knew there was a *chance*.

ALICE

(*Gaily*)

And you're saving three months on the regular route!

ISOLDE

(*Going to* AUGIE *and taking his arm*)

You see, darling? The reward of virtue.

NOVICK

Now remember — no promises, but I'm going to try my best
for you. I think you'd make a wonderful mother, Mrs. Poole.
Now, I'd like to talk to your husband privately for a moment. I
have a few questions to put to him that might prove embarrassing
in front of others. You understand.

ISOLDE

Oh, yes — of course.

(*She goes to door to house, turns, holds up crossed fingers to* AUGIE, *and exits*)

ALICE

(*Rising, calls to* ISOLDE)

I'll call you, darling. Come on, Dick.

(*She goes to* AUGIE *as* DICK *sets glass on bar, and looks at*
AUGIE *thoughtfully*)

We told Miss Novick you're on the wagon.

(*She turns to* NOVICK, *shaking hands*)

Good-by, Miss Novick. It was nice to see you again.

110

NOVICK

Good-by, Mrs. Pepper.

DICK

(*Taking her hand*)
It was more than nice. It was awe-inspiring!
(*They go.* AUGIE *rushes over, closes door and turns back accusingly*)

AUGIE

(*Hoarsely*)
Miss Novick! What the devil did you come here for? What did you mean — you're going to do your *best?*

NOVICK

(*Breaks in, calmly*)
It's perfectly all right, Mr. Poole. There's nothing to get excited about.

AUGIE

Excited! Nothing to get excited about! Do you realize what you're *saying?*

NOVICK

(*Smiles*)
Please — you're much too emotional to discuss it now. Wait till you calm down and think about it objectively.

AUGIE

(*Frantically*)
I'll *never* calm down! And I'll never be objective again as long as I live!
(*Getting hold of himself*)

111

Miss Novick, I realize this is all my fault. And I'm willing to take full responsibility —

NOVICK
(*Breaks in, coolly*)
Thank you, Mr. Poole. Have you got the check?

AUGIE
(*Taking it out of his pocket*)
Yes — here —
(*He hands it to her, taking great care to keep his distance*)
But — the *baby?*

NOVICK
(*Smiles and puts check in her bag*)
I don't think we'll meet again. After my confinement I'm leaving for the Australian Archipelago and I can't take a baby on a field trip.
(*She starts to door*)

AUGIE
I've got a better idea! *You* stay here and *I'll* go to the Archipelago!

NOVICK
(*Laughs and holds out her hand*)
Good-by, Mr. Poole.

AUGIE
(*Violently*)
You haven't answered my questions. The child —

112

NOVICK

Don't suffer so. It's not your fault. In my country we have a proverb that may comfort you.

AUGIE

What is it? I can use anything.

NOVICK

"*Los pisze prosto krzyvymi liniami.*"
(*This is Polish for "Fate writes straight with crooked lines"; however, she does not translate.* AUGIE *nods solemnly as though he understands*)
So don't worry.
(*Crosses to door*)
I'll do what's best for all four of us.

AUGIE

Four of us?

NOVICK

You, your wife, the baby and me.
(*She exits. He stares after her, then turns back into room, a dazed expression on his face.* ISOLDE *hurries in right, very eager*)

ISOLDE

Well? What did she say? Do you think we'll get it?
(*He turns to her slowly*)

AUGIE

(*Fervently*)

It looks that way, darling. All we can do now is *pray*.

CURTAIN FALLS

TIME: *Almost six months later.*

AT RISE: AUGIE *is looking out the window anxiously.* DICK *is in swivel chair looking at cartoons and chuckling to himself. The anniversary plant is now withered and drooping in a bigger jardiniere.*

DICK

(*Chuckling as he reads*)

Augie, this one is swell! The one with the goat in the empty lot eating the copy of Duncan Hines' restaurant guide.

AUGIE

(*Grimly*)

I guess I'm funniest when I'm suffering.

DICK

That's right. As they say, an artist should be tormented but not disturbed.

AUGIE

That's true. Whatever happened to quiet desperation? Do you realize what month this is?

DICK

Sure. It's March.

115

AUGIE

The Ides of March! The net is drawing tighter.

DICK

(*Glances up at last*)

Any returns from upstate?

AUGIE

Nothing since this post card three months ago.
(*Picks up card from shelf and reads it*)
"Still working on it. Best. Estelle Novick."

DICK

(*Admiringly*)

Novick — a giant among women. Well, you've got to give her credit. She didn't have any staff to help her, like Kinsey. She had to do her own research.

AUGIE

Door to door.
(*Bicycle bell sounds.* AUGIE *looks out the window anxiously. Yells*)
Look out! Isolde! Look out! You'll break your neck on that damn bicycle!
(DICK *rises and places cartoon on drawing board as* AUGIE *runs to center door and opens it.* ISOLDE *enters, wearing pedal-pushers and looking flushed and lovely. She carries a loaded market bag.* AUGIE *takes it from her*)
What are you trying to do — riding a bicycle on these slippery roads? And what's more, you don't even know how to ride a bicycle.

ISOLDE

Expectant mothers are supposed to exercise up to the last minute.

AUGIE

(*Unhappily*)

Isolde, *darling* — listen — *please.* You've got to stop building yourself up. A million things can go wrong. We haven't got the kid yet.

ISOLDE

(*Smiles reassuringly*)

It's all right, Augie. I'm prepared for anything. It's just a feeling I have, that's all . . .

AUGIE

(*Nods unhappily*)

Yeah . . . I know those feelings.

(*He feels her hands*)

I'll put this stuff away. You're freezing! I'll make you a cup of coffee.

(*He goes off right*)

ISOLDE

(*Suspiciously*)

He gets sweeter and sweeter.

DICK

Yes. We could all take a lesson from him.

ISOLDE

(*Crosses to sofa and sits, taking a letter out of her pocket*)

117

Oh, Dick. We got the strangest thing in the mail yesterday. The *Townsman* sent us a slip for our tax return and there's a thousand dollars I can't account for.

DICK

(*Smiles weakly*)

In your favor or against you?

ISOLDE

They claim they paid us twelve thousand dollars, and all I can add up is eleven. Maybe *you'd* know about it.

(DICK *takes letter from her and puts on his horn-rimmed glasses*)

I'm so stupid about these things —

DICK

(*He looks it over and whistles*)

Twelve thousand dollars! I didn't realize — that's pretty good for six months.

ISOLDE

(*Rises and crosses to bench*)

Yes . . . but you see, I'm a little confused because we only received eleven.

(*There's a pause as* DICK *studies letter intently, trying to think of something*)

DICK

Oh?

(*An idea. Crosses and hands letter to her*)

I know what that is. They kept a thousand out for the withholding tax.

ISOLDE

(*Flatly, as she puts letter in her pocket and sits on bench*)
No, it couldn't be. We paid the tax ourselves.

DICK

Oh?
(*He takes off glasses, blows on them, and puts them in
coat breast pocket. He smiles ruefully*)
Well, the fact of the matter is, I've been playing the market a
little — you know, those penny Canadian stocks — and I prom-
ised Alice I wouldn't. Well, she was right. I needed a thousand
to get out and Augie came through. I told him not to say anything in front of Alice because she'd blow her top. But he could
have told *you.*

ISOLDE

(*Smiles*)
Oh, of course. So you owe Augie a thousand dollars?

DICK

(*Uneasily*)
Yeah. Never mentioned it, huh?

ISOLDE

(*Smiles*)
I'm sure he thought it was too trivial to mention. But we could
use it now — if you're through with it.

DICK

(*Trapped*)
Sure . . . I'm through with it all right.
(*Brightens*)

Tell you what. I'll give it to Augie.
(AUGIE *enters right, carrying a cup of coffee*)

AUGIE

Here you are, darling.

DICK

(*Hastily*)
Augie, if you get a minute, drop over to the house. I've got something important to show you.
(*He exits*)

AUGIE

Everything with that guy is important.
(*He kisses top of* ISOLDE's *head and starts left*)

ISOLDE

(*Eyeing him as she sips coffee*)
Oh, Augie —
(*He turns*)
I've been trying to figure out my checkbook all morning, but it doesn't balance.

AUGIE

Well, if your check book doesn't balance, then the bank is wrong.
(*Starts left again*)

ISOLDE

I couldn't be a thousand dollars out of the way.
(*He stops dead on "thousand dollars"*)

AUGIE

(*Swallows*)

A thousand? Even?

ISOLDE

(*Eyes him*)

To the penny.

AUGIE

Well, the bank's closed. . . . Why don't you wait until to-morrow and call them?

ISOLDE

I *did* call them, this morning. There's no mistake, Augie.
   (*He looks at her a moment, thinking fast, then smiles boyishly*)

AUGIE

I guess I'd better come clean —

ISOLDE

(*Coolly, lifting her eyebrows*)

Yes?

AUGIE

(*Laughs*)

"Oh, what a tangled web we weave when first we practice to deceive." Who was it said that?

ISOLDE

(*Flatly*)

The cashier at the Westport National Bank.

121

AUGIE

The truth is, before I ever signed with the *Townsman,* I'd been borrowing from Dick. Oh, fifty here and twenty there — pocket money. You know how it mounts up.

ISOLDE

Of course — to a thousand.

AUGIE

I didn't want to go to you for it —

ISOLDE

So you went to Dick?
(He nods)
You two boys certainly go to bat for each other, don't you?

AUGIE
(Nobly)

What are friends for?
(He goes to her with that boyish smile, sits on bench)
I should have told you this before. I guess it was my silly pride.

ISOLDE

(We have a feeling she didn't go for it, but she's playing along)
It was silly, Augie. You know anything we have is ours together.

AUGIE
(Kisses her cheek)

I know that, darling —
(He rises, facing away from her)

122

— but every time I had to go to you for anything I felt like a hopeless failure.

(*He waits for the phrase to have its usual effect, but this time it doesn't. She's thoughtful, as though she knows he's lying*)

Isolde, you're not listening.

ISOLDE
(*Coolly*)

Oh, yes, I am.

(*She rises, crosses right to door*)

I heard every word. . . . You felt like a hopeless failure.

(*She exits quietly*)

AUGIE

Yes. Well?

(*He turns, opening his arms. He looks at closed door, stunned.* DICK *looks in window, shakes sleigh bells slightly to get* AUGIE's *attention*)

AUGIE
(*Crossing to sofa*)

Come on in! I was just going to call you.

DICK
(*Coming through window*)

I was just going to call you, but you had to get one of those lousy phones — you might as well be on television. Now, let's get this story straight. I told Isolde you lent me a grand to cover up some stock losses.

(Crosses down in front of sofa)

AUGIE

(Clutches his head)

Oh, my God!

DICK

Don't worry — she swallowed it.

AUGIE

(Wails)

I told her *you* lent *me* a thousand.

DICK

Then it won't stay down.

(An idea hits him)

All right, I'll tell her I was covering up for you, because I didn't know you told her you'd borrowed from me. Right?

AUGIE

(Sits wearily on sofa)

Not even *Alice* would go for that.

DICK

No, she wouldn't.

(He sits, too)

This is getting to be a Kafka nightmare. And what's more, I'm supposed to give you a thousand dollars.

AUGIE

Give it to me and I'll hold it until this blows over.

DICK

Give it to you? If I gave you a check for a thousand dollars, it'd bounce from Westport to Port Arthur.

AUGIE

(*Rising*)

This is all I needed! Dick, you don't know what I'm going through! Now everything I *say* she thinks is a lie.

(*He crosses to plant*)

Here I am — the symbol of Augie Poole. I got a bigger jardiniere, and look at the shape I'm in.

(*Holds the sorry-looking plant aloft. The phone rings.* AUGIE *crosses and presses button*)

Hello?

MC CRACKEN'S VOICE

Mr. Poole?

AUGIE

Yes?

MC CRACKEN

This is Miss McCracken of Rock-a-bye.

(AUGIE *and* DICK *exchange terrified looks*)

AUGIE

(*Weakly*)

Where — *where* did you say you're from?

125

MC CRACKEN

Rock-a-bye. Aren't you Mr. *August* Poole?

AUGIE

(*Sinks into swivel chair, staring at* DICK)

Yes — yes, this is August Poole —

MC CRACKEN

(*Very cheerfully*)

Well, I have some very exciting news for you. Is Mrs. Poole there?

AUGIE

(*Helplessly, looking at Dick*)

No. She's not here at the moment.

(*Weakly*)

Can I take a message?

MC CRACKEN

No, I think you'd both better hear it together. I'm in the village right now. I have a few stops. I'll drop in later — say four o'clock?

AUGIE

(*Swallows*)

Yes — sure — of course. Thanks, Miss McCracken.

(*He switches off phone, nods grimly*)

The Ides of March.

DICK

(*Unconvincingly*)

Maybe it's just in the offing — a prospect — nothing definite. Maybe it's not even your baby.

AUGIE

(*Miserably*)

No, it's mine all right. I can feel it! I swear I'm going crazy! Suppose Isolde finds out? What'll she do?

DICK

How is she going to find out?

AUGIE

You know Isolde. She's smart — she's too *damn* smart. Her intuition is terrifying. You've played The Game with her. She knows the answer before you've acted out the first lousy syllable.

DICK

(*Nods*)

That's true. She's bewitched.

AUGIE

It'd be different if it were Alice. She wouldn't tumble if you brought a dame home and kept her in the Deepfreeze.

DICK

Thank God!

AUGIE

I was never cut out to lead a double life. I can't even lead a *single* life.

DICK

Augie, stop crucifying yourself. You're not to blame. Name me one creative person who wasn't a son-of-a-bitch.

127

AUGIE

(*Thinks a moment*)

Louisa May Alcott.

DICK

(*Ignores this*)

Balzac, Gauguin, Wagner, Dumas, Dickens, Lautrec — all impossible!

AUGIE

(*Pays no attention. Rises*)

And the terrible thing is, I'm torn. I *want* that baby.

DICK

(*Staring*)

What?

AUGIE

(*Defiantly, crossing to* DICK)

Why not? It's my child, isn't it? It's a perfectly natural thing to want your own child, isn't it?

DICK

(*Shakes his head*)

That way lies madness, my boy!

AUGIE

If it were my child by a former marriage, nobody would think anything of it.

DICK

(*Nods thoughtfully*)

That's reasonable. Maybe it *is* best to come clean and tell her everything. Confession is good for the soul.

128

AUGIE

Only in the sense that a tweed coat is good for dandruff.

DICK

She's intelligent — broad-minded —

AUGIE

The sands at Las Vegas are littered with the bodies of guys who thought their wives were broad-minded.

DICK

What are you going to tell her?

AUGIE

(*Very agitated*)
Maybe I won't tell her anything. Maybe I'll let McCracken break the news first. Why jump the gun? Oh, my God — intrigue is not for me!
(ISOLDE *comes from house, very excited*)

ISOLDE

(*At sofa*)
Dr. Vancouver just dropped by. He has another lead for us —
(*They look at her eagerly*)

AUGIE

He *has? What?*

ISOLDE

There's a young girl in the village — she's only eighteen —

DICK

The ideal age for adoption.

ISOLDE

(*Sitting on sofa*)

No. She's a girl Dr. Vancouver's been taking care of. She had a romance with some boy who can't marry her.

AUGIE

Amazing! Until you get into this thing you don't realize how much of that is going on.

ISOLDE

He thinks maybe he can arrange it for us.

DICK

Great! That would solve *everything!*
(*She looks at him surprised. He rises nervously*)
I mean — you wouldn't have to be investigated and all that nonsense.

ISOLDE

He says she's a very healthy girl from a good family. And the man certainly must be all right. He's a cadet at West Point.

DICK

A fine American boy!

ISOLDE

That's why he can't marry her. It seems that cadets are broken out if they marry before they graduate.

AUGIE

(*Nervously*)

When is she going to have it?

ISOLDE

Any day now.

DICK

(*Rubbing his hands*)

That sounds like your best bet to me — a lovely, healthy local girl and a strapping young Army man! How could you do better?

ISOLDE

(*Torn*)

I suppose so, but it doesn't seem fair to Rock-a-bye.

AUGIE

(*Alarmed*)

Now, Isolde, don't start cooking up a maternal feeling for an institution!

ISOLDE

Well, after all, we owe them something. They were the first to accept us.

DICK

You don't owe them a damn thing!

(*Pacing*)

Sending investigators snooping at your bankroll, sniffing at your friends — and pinching you like fruit to see if you're ripe.

AUGIE

He's right. You can't go accepting and rejecting a baby like some damn magazine editor. "This one has some interesting parts, but it's not quite what we're looking for." We're going to take the first baby that pops up.

ISOLDE

(*Rises and crosses to door right*)

I'll gladly take the first baby that pops up. Make me a Martini, will you, dear?

(*She exits into house*)

DICK

You better start pulling for that dark horse from West Point.

AUGIE

(*Crosses to bar moodily*)

There's only one thing. I've always hated the brass ever since I was in the Army.

DICK

(*Crosses to join him at bar.* AUGIE *picks up gin bottle*)

He's not brass. He's just a poor unlucky kid who got caught. You don't know how lucky you are. This boy's undoubedly a very high type — intelligent, healthy, alert. West Point? He could be President some day.

AUGIE

(*Pouring gin into cocktail pitcher*)

What's so hot about a guy who'll get a girl of eighteen in trouble when he knows he can't marry her?

DICK

Stone-casting is not your métier, my friend.

AUGIE

Mine is an entirely different situation!

DICK

Different or not, you ought to be grateful to the boy instead of picking on him.

AUGIE

(*Flourishing swizzle stick*)
Why should I give this jerk preference over my own kid?
(*Stirs briskly*)

DICK

What's *wrong* with you? Are you *asking* for trouble?

AUGIE

I'm pretty healthy and alert and intelligent myself — and I didn't go to West Point on a letter from my idiot Congressman!
(*Pours two drinks*)

DICK

(*After a long pause, staring at him*)
I see — *your own* child. That's becoming an obsession, isn't it?
(AUGIE *nods*)
You go to the Bible for inspiration. Let me remind you of something. When Daniel got out of the lions' den, he did not go back for his hat!
(DICK *holds glasses aloft as* AUGIE *picks up vermouth bottle with atomizer and squirts some in each drink*)
Easy on the vermouth!
(ALICE *enters, closing door, unpregnant and svelte for the first time*)

133

ALICE

I thought you were going to make me a new batch of formula.

DICK

I will, dear —

(*Raises glass*)

— one batch of formula at a time.

(*Sets glass on bar, smiling warmly as he crosses to her*)

What a lovely dress, darling!

ALICE

(*Wards him off*)

Yes — and this time I'm going to get some wear out of it!

AUGIE

(*Crosses to door right, carrying Martini*)

I thought you two were going to Lake Placid for a week.

DICK

We can't. The sitter's in Bermuda.

AUGIE

I wouldn't mind sitting in Bermuda right now myself. Excuse me — I want to take this to Isolde.

(*He goes into house.* ALICE *looks after him narrowly*)

ALICE

There he goes *again*, waiting on her hand and foot. Poor Isolde.

DICK

Why "poor Isolde?"

134

ALICE

Isn't it perfectly obvious? He's got someone, and he's trying to cover up by giving service.

DICK

Ohhh. Well, if that's the way your mind works, make your own formula!

ALICE

I think it's shocking. Don't you?
(*He takes cigarette from coffee table*)

DICK

I don't sit in judgment on anybody.
(*Lights it*)

ALICE

Oh? Maybe you're just trying to pave the way for the future?

DICK

What does *that* mean?

ALICE

When you might have an affair of your own some day?

DICK

We were talking about Augie. How did this suddenly boomerang to me?

ALICE

Never mind. But any time you want to hole up in town with some fleabag, you go right ahead!

DICK

Hole up *in* town *with a* floozy *in* a fleabag! I wish you'd get terms like that straight. It reflects on me.
(*Sits on daybed*)

ALICE
(*Looking towards door right*)
Poor Isolde.
(AUGIE *enters.* ALICE *stares at him with sudden new interest, as though she has never seen him before. He's aware of it and becomes self-conscious*)

AUGIE

What's the matter? Lipstick on my face?
(*He takes out handkerchief and wipes mouth*)
Isolde kissed me when I brought her the drink. She does it all the time — instead of a tip. She never has change.
(*Gives* ALICE *a worried glance*)

ALICE
(*Still staring at* AUGIE)
Dick, would you run over and see if the baby's all right?

DICK
(*Flatly*)
No.

AUGIE
(*Gives* DICK *a shocked look and starts to go*)
I'll go over, Alice.

ALICE

(*Shooting* DICK *a look*)
Never mind. It's not important.

DICK

She doesn't want *you* to go. She just wants *me* to go. Forget
it, darling. I'm not leaving your side.
(AUGIE *looks at them in bewilderment as* ISOLDE *enters
carrying the Martini*)

ISOLDE

What kind of Martini is this? A secret weapon? I like a little
vermouth in my gin.

AUGIE

It's strictly regulation — nine to one.

ISOLDE

Oh, by the way, I spoke to Alice. She's going to give me a
check for the thousand dollars.
(DICK *rises*)

AUGIE

What!

ALICE

Richard, you ought to be ashamed of yourself — after you
gave me your solemn word of honor that you wouldn't fool
around in the market.
(*She looks at* ISOLDE)

This is a new phase — lying to me!

(*She goes out.* DICK *is speechless. He looks slowly from* ISOLDE *to* AUGIE. *Passes his hand over his chin as he stares at* AUGIE *a stunned moment and then exits slowly, leaving door open.* ISOLDE *breaks the tension by crossing to* AUGIE *with Martini glass held out to him. He takes it and goes to bar as she follows*)

ISOLDE

Augie, tell me the truth. What really did happen to that thousand dollars?

(*He rattles her glass against cocktail pitcher as he pours Martini back into it*)

Dick got into trouble, didn't he? And you're covering up for him.

AUGIE

(*Picks up vermouth*)

No, no! Nothing like that.

(*Pulls atomizer out of vermouth bottle and pours vermouth into cocktail pitcher*)

ISOLDE

What was it? A woman?

AUGIE

When a man's in trouble, why does a woman always take it for granted that it's another woman? Don't you have any more respect for one another than that?

ISOLDE

Very well, then, what was it?

AUGIE

(*Stirring the Martini*)

I'm sorry — it wouldn't be honorable for us to go into this any further.

ISOLDE

(*Looking at him*)

I must say, you men have a strong union.

AUGIE

We need one if we're going to stay in business with women.
(*He pours her drink*)

ISOLDE

(*Takes drink, looks at him*)

I love you for defending him, but do you think he'd ever do that for you?

AUGIE

(*Startled*)

Huh? Why would he have to?

ISOLDE

That's one thing I never have to worry about with you.
(*Turning away*)

Poor Alice. But I guess Dick can't help it. It's what I told you — he's got to keep proving himself.

AUGIE

That's what I like about you. Your understanding of other people.

ISOLDE

Thank you, dear.

AUGIE

Not just the Peppers, but everything. Like the time that investigator was here —

ISOLDE

Miss Novick —

AUGIE

Uh-huh. And you said bad girls never get into trouble.
(*He gives her a sidelong glance*)
That was *so* perceptive.

ISOLDE
(*At fireplace*)

Well, it's true.

AUGIE

(*Follows her, closes outside door*)
And, of course, the same holds for the man in the case?

ISOLDE

(*Peering into fireplace*)
Soot! We must have that fireplace cleaned.

AUGIE

(*Louder, moving to her*)
I say, the same holds for the *man?*

140

ISOLDE

Well, that depends.

AUGIE

On what?

ISOLDE

(*Turning*)

The circumstances.

AUGIE

(*Quickly*)

Of course! You mean the very fact that they could have blundered into such a muddle *proves* their innocence —

(*He sits on bench*)

Babes in the wood.

ISOLDE

This is a new tack for you. You used to be so critical of men of that type.

AUGIE

Well, I'm beginning to see things *your* way. "To know all is to forgive all."

ISOLDE

The prospect of fatherhood is softening you up already.

AUGIE

(*Earnestly*)

Isolde, darling — please — don't joke. This is terribly important for me. I never felt less worthy of you or needed you more than I do now.

141

ISOLDE

(*Stands behind him, arms around him, face next to his*)

Augie — darling — you sound as though something terrible were going to happen to us. Nothing's going to happen. We're happily married and we're going to stay that way.

AUGIE

Let's make a pact right now!

ISOLDE

(*Laughs*)

All right — a pact.

AUGIE

Let's shake on it!

(*They kiss*)

I guess people deserve what they get in this life, but I want to deserve what I've *got*.

(*He kisses her again and they snuggle as* DICK *comes in, closing door*)

DICK

What? In broad daylight?

AUGIE

(*Shrugs*)

The girl adores me.

(*To* ISOLDE)

You mustn't, darling. Don't make an idol of me.

THE TUNNEL OF LOVE

ISOLDE

(*Goes to door, taking Martini*)

I know — feet of clay.

(*She goes*)

AUGIE

(*His smile dies*)

It isn't my feet that are made of clay. It's my head.

(*Rising*)

How can I take a chance on losing a wonderful girl like that! I've got to get a kid from another source — a baby that's a total stranger.

DICK

You'd better start working on it. It's almost four o'clock. That character from Rock-a-bye'll be here any minute.

AUGIE

I've got one chance left. That West Point entry. Dr. Vancouver up!

DICK

Better call him and get the odds. It's almost post time.

(AUGIE *crosses to phone and dials decisively, five numbers*)

VANCOUVER'S VOICE

Dr. Vancouver speaking.

AUGIE

Doctor, I'm calling to find out about that couple you told my

143

wife about. You know — that West Point cadet who got that eighteen-year-old girl in trouble?

VANCOUVER'S VOICE

(*Very annoyed*)

Who *is* this?

AUGIE

This is Mr. Poole. I've got to know something right away. How soon is she expecting?

VANCOUVER'S VOICE

Well, Mr. Poole, as a matter of fact, the whole situation has changed since I talked to your wife.

AUGIE

Changed?

VANCOUVER'S VOICE

Yes. The boy has agreed to marry her as soon as he graduates, and his parents have agreed to take care of her until then. I was going to call Mrs. Poole, but I've been tied up here.

AUGIE

Thanks, Doctor. I'll tell her.

(*He switches off phone*)

Scratched! Like I said — the Fates.

DICK

Double-crossing quack! *That's* gonna be a happy marriage. A gold bar on his shoulder and a three-year-old kid on his lap!

(*Crosses to phone*)

144

Well, what other leads have we got? How do we call the Cradle?

(*He starts to dial.* AUGIE *grabs his hand*)

AUGIE

Keep your hands off that phone.

(*He sighs and picks up Scotch bottle*)

Well, I'm going to take this lying down.

(DICK *joins him. As* AUGIE *pours second drink, there is a knock at the door*)

AUGIE

(*Looks at watch*)

Never ask for whom the bell tolls.

(*They drink simultaneously. Without looking at* DICK, AUGIE *crosses and opens door.* MISS MC CRACKEN, *a bright-eyed, birdlike woman of about thirty-eight beams in on them. Door remains open*)

MC CRACKEN

Mr. Poole?

(*He nods, baring his neck to the Fates*)

How do you do? I'm Miss McCracken from Rock-a-bye.

AUGIE

Come in, Miss McCracken. This is Mr. Pepper.

MC CRACKEN

(*Crossing to shake hands with* DICK)

Pepper? Pepper? Oh, yes, you're the reference for the Pooles.

145

AUGIE

Miss McCracken, won't you sit down?

MC CRACKEN

(*She sits on sofa*)

Thank you.

AUGIE

You have some news for us, Miss McCracken?

MC CRACKEN

I'll wait and tell it to both of you together.

AUGIE

I'll call my wife.
(*He goes to door to house and calls*)
Isolde! Isolde!

DICK

(*Eyes her thoughtfully*)

Frankly, Miss McCracken, I wish they'd sent *you* here in the first place.

ISOLDE

(*Offstage*)

What is it, Augie?

AUGIE

Can you come here a minute?

ISOLDE

(*Offstage*)

I'll be right there.

146

AUGIE

(*Coming back to center*)

She'll be right here.

(MC CRACKEN *watches him with slight smile. He smiles
back uncomfortably. She laughs; he chuckles; her laughter
grows.* ISOLDE *comes in from house, trailed by* ALICE)

This is my wife. Dear, this is Miss McCracken from Rock-a-bye.

MC CRACKEN

(*Rises and reaches to shake hands*)

How do you do?

ISOLDE

Rock-a-bye. This is Mrs. Pepper, our reference. Oh! What is it,
Miss McCracken? Please!

MC CRACKEN

(*Not to be rushed*)

First things first.

(*They all sit*)

Now, let me say, Mrs. Poole, we go to great lengths at Rock-a-
bye to match the right child with the right parents —

ISOLDE

(*Impatiently*)

Yes, yes! I know!

MC CRACKEN

And yesterday we received a baby we think might be the very
one for you two people.

147

ISOLDE

Oh ...

MC CRACKEN

Naturally, I can't give you any details, but as it happens, I know the mother very well. She just completed her thesis and won her doctor's degree in science.

ISOLDE

Imagine, Augie — a Doctor of Science.

DICK

(*Nods solemnly*)
Science, the scourge of mankind.

MC CRACKEN

I understand the father is a decent sort, but somewhat weak and irresponsible.
(AUGIE *nods solemnly*)
It was one of those brief, unhappy love affairs in which one of the partners, unfortunately, was married.

ISOLDE

Luckily for us!

ALICE

It's an ill wind!

ISOLDE

Please, Miss McCracken, tell me, what is it? A girl or a boy? Not that we care! We'll take *anything!*

148

MC CRACKEN

A lovely, healthy boy — six and a half pounds — with red curly hair and big brown eyes.

(*She looks at* AUGIE)

Just made to order for you!

(*She breaks into laughter*)

ISOLDE

A boy, darling! A boy, with red curly hair! And big brown eyes!

AUGIE

(*Stares out into space*)

It's a boy . . .

ISOLDE

When can we get him?

MC CRACKEN

Today, if you like.

ISOLDE

If we *like?* Augie! Come on!

(*Rises*)

ALICE

(*Rises*)

Can we go along?

ISOLDE

We *want* you, darling!

149

ALICE

We'll take our station wagon! The heater's fixed now. Dick, get the station wagon out!

(*He rises mechanically and nods, looking at* AUGIE, *who looks straight ahead with a stunned expression.* ALICE *goes to door*)

I'll fix up a basket with some bunting.

ISOLDE

(*Running after her*)

No, *I'll* do it!

(*Calls back over her shoulder*)

Miss McCracken, meet you at the car!

(*They're off right*)

MC CRACKEN

(*Beams after her, rises*)

This is the best part of my job — telling the new mothers and dads. She looks so radiant.

(*Turns to* AUGIE)

But, you — you look stunned. That's typical. You must have made quite an impression at headquarters, Mr. Poole!

AUGIE

(*Weakly, rises*)

I did? Why?

MC CRACKEN

There were almost two hundred couples ahead of you, and all at once *your* name jumped up to the top of the list.

(*Automobile horn sounds*)

You're a lucky man, Mr. Poole — a mighty lucky man! There's a tremendous demand for our little ones, and a very small supply.
(*She goes out*)

AUGIE

(*He starts to door, and stops*)
You've got to admit one thing.

DICK

What?

AUGIE

I finally licked the law of supply and demand.
(*They go out as —*)

CURTAIN FALLS

ACT THREE

ACT THREE

TIME: *A month later; a beautiful, sunny morning.*

AT RISE: *The center door is open. A bassinet is standing directly center stage. A baby's lusty cry pierces the stillness. After a few moments,* AUGIE *hurries in from outside, holding a putter in his hand. He goes to bassinet anxiously. He now has a moustache.*

AUGIE

What's the matter, son? Take it easy, boy.
> (*The cries get louder*)

Hold it, hold it! Momma isn't home! Now don't start anything!
> (*He goes out center door and calls loudly*)

Alice! Alice, can you come over? Right away?

ALICE'S VOICE
(*Off*)

What is it?

AUGIE

The baby — *quick!*
> (*He turns back to baby and looks in at him helplessly*)

Sh! Sh!
> (*An especially loud angry wail*)

For God's sake, sh!

155

(*Sings frantically*)
"I'm piggy-back Jack, I'm piggy-back Jill, the Paper-Mate Pen
with the built-in refill!"
(ALICE *rushes in*)

ALICE

What's the matter? What's wrong?

AUGIE

He won't stop crying! Look at him! He's turning blue!

ALICE

(*Smiles and shakes her head, leaning over bassinet*)
He's not blue — he's pink — and he's probably just hungry.
When did he have his last bottle?
(AUGIE *remembers and looks at his watch quickly*)

AUGIE

That's right! Sure! I never thought of that.
(*He runs over to the bar where there is a hot plate, bot-
tles, and other equipment laid out on a towel, such as nip-
ples, pins, and so on*)
I'll heat the formula.
(*Appears to plug in hot-plate cord under bar*)
Coming up, my little friend. Just a couple of seconds on the
fire . . .

ALICE

(*Looking at him*)
Don't you keep a schedule of the feedings?

AUGIE

Yeah, but I keep forgetting to mark it down. He finished a fifth about an hour ago.

(*Slaps his forehead*)

I don't know what's the matter with me. I can't retain anything for two minutes.

(DICK *comes in from outside. The wails have subsided to a few sleepy hiccups*)

DICK

Well, what was it?

ALICE

Nothing. Hunger pangs.

DICK

(*He drops hat and newspaper on daybed*)

I almost called out the Fire Department, the way you were hollering.

AUGIE

If I'm going to panic I can't keep my voice down.

ALICE

Call me for the next emergency.

AUGIE

I'm sorry. Thanks, Alice.

(ALICE *goes to* DICK)

ALICE

Oh, Dick — when you go into the village, will you get me some egg foo young and some seedless grapes.

DICK

Sure, and thanks for not waiting till two o'clock in the morning.
(ALICE *kisses him and goes out*)

AUGIE

What's that?

DICK

Alice is off to the races again.

AUGIE

Congratulations.

DICK

Shut up. How are you coming along with the new gags?

AUGIE

I haven't been able to think of anything funny in days.

DICK

(*Crossing to bench*)
Listen, I've got a deadline to meet. I'm way behind. Nothing good has come in.

AUGIE

The hell with *your* deadline! I'm going crazy here! I'm all screwed up —
(*The baby cries again*)
Now you've woke the baby with your damn shop talk!
(*He takes bottle out of warming pan*)

THE TUNNEL OF LOVE

DICK

(*Sitting on bench*)

I've had four kids and nobody's ever seen *me* go into a tailspin.

AUGIE

(*Shakes few drops inside his wrist, tastes it*)

Perfect.

(*Crosses to baby as he talks*)

You're going to love this today, Augie. A brand-new taste sensation.

(*Puts bottle in bassinet. Baby stops crying abruptly and makes contented gurgling sounds*)

We cut down on the corn syrup and added a dash of Angostura bitters. Here, wrap your gums around that.

(*More baby sounds*)

Isn't that good? I knew you'd go for it.

(*Final gurgle from baby. He smiles tenderly*)

I could stand here all day and just watch him — sleeping, breathing — the wonder of it.

DICK

(*Shakes his head*)

Can this transcendent soul be the Augie Poole I knew?

AUGIE

Don't mock. It takes an experience like this to make you understand the spiritual values of life.

159

DICK

Very touching. Okay, he's quiet. How about some gags?

AUGIE

I can't, I tell you! How can I dream up gags at a time like this? I thought maybe when the baby came Isolde'd be so wrapped up she'd forget about everything else. But it's *worse*.

DICK

Why?

AUGIE

I'm jumpy — and *she's* jumpy — you can see she's *thinking* all the time. I tell you I don't like it when she's thinking.

DICK

About what?

AUGIE

That thousand bucks, for one thing. Every once in a while she makes a crack — and then she looks in the crib — and then she looks at me — and back to the crib —
    (*He demonstrates, swiveling his head sharply*)
Like at Wimbledon.

DICK

(*Nods*)
I can imagine. I just got a flash of the kid. The resemblance is frightening.

AUGIE

And your idea — this lousy moustache — hasn't helped. Just makes me look ridiculous.

160

DICK

Maybe we should have tried sideburns.

(AUGIE *gives him a terrible look, then turns to baby*)

AUGIE

Ah, he's out like a light — not a sound. He sleeps like a Cadillac.

(*Takes the half-empty bottle from bassinet*)

DICK

Heard anything from La Novick?

AUGIE

(*Shakes his head*)

I wrote her a letter, after the baby came, asking if there was anything I could do.

DICK

You've done all you can.

AUGIE

(*Crosses to sofa*)

My God, here I end up adopting my own flesh and blood, like the hero in some Greek tragedy.

DICK

It's given you a kind of stature. I see you now wrapped in classic irony. Prometheus, chained to a rock —

AUGIE

(*Nods sadly, holding up bottle*)

Prometheus and Son.

161

DICK

(*Rising*)

We've got to do something to get Isolde's mind off that resemblance.

AUGIE

(*Bitterly*)

What do you propose? Grow a moustache on the baby?

DICK

I'll give a party —

AUGIE

(*Sits on sofa*)

Just what I need — a *party!*

DICK

(*Ignores this, crosses to sofa*)

We'll invite all the couples we know who've adopted children. Must be half a dozen. There are some strange similarities. The Crowleys' girl — and that kid of the Marshalls looks an awful lot like Ted. We'll give a prize to the couple whose kid looks most like them —

AUGIE

And I'll win the prize hands down. Brilliant!

DICK

No, you won't, because I'll be the judge — and I'll put the fix in and give the prize to Ted Marshall. Then Isolde will realize this fancied resemblance is a figment of her imagination.

162

AUGIE

(*Shakes his head, rises*)
You'll be the judge, and *you'll* put the fix in, and *that's* going to impress Isolde? Oh, you silly bastard!
(ISOLDE *enters from outside, carrying a package of new diapers. She goes to crib*)

ISOLDE

How is he? Oh, my darling little boy!
(*She looks at baby, then* AUGIE, *then the baby, and back to* AUGIE)
How's he been?

AUGIE

Fine.
(*He crosses and takes diapers from her.* ISOLDE *stares at him intently*)
What is it?

ISOLDE

Nothing. . . . I can't get used to that moustache.

DICK

(*Trying to be cheerful*)
I like it. I think it gives him a look of distinction.

AUGIE

(*Tries to laugh*)
Who knows? I may be grabbed for a gin-and-tonic ad. Where'll I put this — on the bar?

ISOLDE

No. In the nursery.

(*He takes diapers and bottle off right*)

DICK

(*Nervously — he doesn't want to be alone with* ISOLDE)
Well, I'll run along —
(*He starts out, making a wide detour around the bassinet
to door, where he picks up his hat*)

ISOLDE

(*Sweetly*)
What's the matter, Dick? Don't you want to see him?

DICK

(*Turns*)
See who?

ISOLDE

The baby. You seem to make a wide arc around him every time
you come over here.

DICK

(*Unconvincingly, as he puts hat on daybed and takes
glasses out of breast pocket*)
Of course I want to see him!
(*He laughs and goes over to the bassinet and peers in.
His smile fades and he stares, fascinated. He puts on glasses
and bends over for a closer look*)

ISOLDE

(*Softly*)
Who do you think he looks like?

DICK
(Straightens up)

Churchill.

(He takes off glasses. ALICE *comes in from outside, carrying that new dress of Act II on a hanger)*

ALICE

Hello, darling. Look —
(She holds up dress)
I've got a present for you — you admired it so —

ISOLDE
(Crosses to her)
What? Your new dress? Why? Don't you like it?

ALICE
(Looks at DICK*)*
Sure I like it. I *love* it! But if I let it out I'll ruin it.

ISOLDE
(Taking dress from ALICE *)*
Alice, not again?

DICK
(Nods heavily)
Maybe we should move to Canada, where they give prizes for this sort of thing.

*(*ISOLDE *lays dress down.* ALICE *goes to bassinet.* ISOLDE *stands at her shoulder)*

ALICE

How is he? Oh, he's sleeping.

"Where did you come from, baby dear?
Out of the everywhere into the here.

(AUGIE *enters from house.* ALICE *looks up at him. Her voice trails off in amazement*)

"Where did you get those big brown — "

It's remarkable. . . . The girls are right. . . . Ever since the baby shower at the club yesterday I've had nothing but phone calls, raving about little Augie!

AUGIE

(*Smiles eagerly*)

Yeah? What did they say?

ALICE

They all said he was such a darling — never cried — just looked up at them with that funny little crooked smile. Just the way *you're* smiling now!

(*His smile freezes*)

And they couldn't get over the resemblance.

(*To* ISOLDE)

It's remarkable!

(*Turns to bassinet*)

ISOLDE

(*Watching* AUGIE)

Yes, it's uncanny.

166

AUGIE

(*Crossing to bassinet*)

I think he looks much more like Isolde. Look at that little nose.
And that mouth — exactly like hers.

ALICE

Not at all! His mouth is much more like yours —
(*She puts a finger over* AUGIE'S *moustache*)

Look!

AUGIE

(*Ducks to escape finger*)

I think I'll put him out in the sun.
(*He rolls bassinet out center door to just outside window*)

DICK

(*Nervously*)

Well, I'll get going —

ISOLDE

(*With a strange air*)

Don't go. I want to show you something. You, too, Alice. I
want you to tell me what you think of this picture. It's a snapshot
I just had enlarged.
(*She takes it from table and hands it to* DICK. ALICE *sits
on bench and* DICK *joins her, handing her the picture*)

ALICE

Cute!

DICK

(*Heartily*)

Good of him, too. Even I can tell from one look at the nipper.

AUGIE

(*Comes in, stands behind them*)

This from the new batch I took, dear? I didn't know you got them back.

(*They smile together*)

ISOLDE

(*Eyeing* AUGIE)

Think it's a good likeness?

ALICE

Perfect, bless his little heart!

DICK

Best I've seen.

ISOLDE

(*Grimly*)

That's very interesting, because it isn't a picture of little Augie at all. It's a picture of *big* Augie, some years ago — when he was little Augie's age.

ALICE

(*Stares*)

No! You're not serious?

(ISOLDE *nods, looking at* AUGIE)

AUGIE
(*Weakly*)
Where'd you get it?

ISOLDE
(*Evenly, crossing below sofa*)
Your mother sent it. She ran across it last week and thought I might like to have it.
(*She turns*)
She said if I showed it to you it'd probably make you blush. . . . You're not blushing at all — you're pale.

AUGIE
I am?

DICK
(*A hollow laugh*)
Old Augie. What do you know?

ISOLDE
I know this. Maybe we all *imagine* the baby looks like Augie, but don't tell me it's my imagination that Augie looked exactly like that baby when he was the same age.

AUGIE
(*Crossing to her*)
Isolde, darling, I love you.
(*She backs away*)

ISOLDE
He's your child, isn't he?

169

(DICK *and* ALICE *rise.* ISOLDE *backs further*)
Isn't he?
(AUGIE *drops his head and spreads his hands*)

AUGIE

(*Brokenly, following her*)

Isolde, darling —

ISOLDE

I know — you love me — and you're a poor, helpless little boy.
Oh, when I think of what a pitiful fool I've been!

AUGIE

Dick — Alice — would you please go?
(*They start to door,* ALICE *leaving picture on bench*)

ISOLDE

(*Stopping them*)

No! Let them stay! From now on you have nothing to say to
me. How could I have deluded myself all these years! My kind,
gentle, honorable husband! I never want to see you again —
you — you lecherous leprechaun!

ALICE

But, darling — you're not being fair — you're condemning the
poor boy without giving him a chance.

ISOLDE

He had his chance and he took it! I'm through with you and
Westport and everybody in it!
(*She goes into house*)

170

BLACKOUT

(*Lights come up on* AUGIE *with drink, which he has picked up from coffee table during blackout*)

AUGIE

Ah, well — maybe it's true what they say. Whom the gods love they punish.
(*He lifts glass, looking up*)
Thanks, boys, I didn't know you cared.
(*He crosses to window*)
Well, I'm not going to stand here and get steam-rollered. I'm going to fight! I went through too much to have that baby.
(*He looks through window at baby*)
Sleeping. Sleep while you can, son. They won't give you a chance when you grow up. Treasure each moment now. This is what you'll be nostalgic for.

DICK

(*Entering carefully, leaving door open*)
She still here?
(AUGIE *nods*)
Good. Then you still have a fighting chance. Augie, in a way I feel responsible for this whole thing. Why don't you let me have a talk with Isolde?

AUGIE

Yes. With your record you're the perfect one to do it. Just stay away from her.
(*Goes to electric razor*)

171

DICK

Okay. Stand there and be plowed under.
(*Starts back to door*)

AUGIE

All I need is time.

DICK

Time for what?

AUGIE

Time to convince her how much we need each other.
(*He plugs in razor*)

DICK

Okay, good luck.
(*He turns away. At sound of razor, he turns back to*
AUGIE, *who is now shaving, looking in mirror on wall over*
bar)
You know, you're foolish to shave that off. It gives you character.

AUGIE

(*Turning, right side of moustache gone*)
It's unfair! You pick them up and toss them away like used
razor blades! But me — just *once* my foot slips, and they nail me
to the wall like a butterfly!

DICK

(*Comes back.* AUGIE *shaves left side of moustache and*
unplugs razor)

172

You're right. There's no justice. But you made the fatal mistake
— you reformed. The unregenerate butterfly flits from flower to
flower without a care in the world.

AUGIE

Without a *what?* Why, you sat right there and moaned to me
about your terrible guilt feelings.

DICK

Oh, didn't I tell you? I've finished my analysis. I'm completely
cured. I can have an affair any time I like and it doesn't bother
me a damn bit!
(*He puts on his hat and exits jauntily, closing door.*
AUGIE *puts razor on bar.* ISOLDE *enters with her two bags*)

ISOLDE
(*Icily*)
I sent for a taxi —

AUGIE

Darling, let me have five minutes — I must talk to you —

ISOLDE

What can you say in five minutes or five years that can convince me of anything? I'll let you know where to send the rest of
my things.
(*She starts off*)

AUGIE

(*Crossing toward her*)
Isolde, I just want to say this. I love you and I love him, and
no matter what happens, I'll bring him up the best way I can.

173

ISOLDE

(*Hand on door*)

You keep your hands off that child! Do you think I'd let you bring him up? You — his father!

(*She goes into house. He starts to follow, but there is a knock at the door. He opens it, revealing* MISS MC CRACKEN)

AUGIE

Miss McCracken!

MC CRACKEN

(*Shaking hands*)

Good afternoon, Mr. Poole.

(*She beams*)

I just peeped in at your little boy. He's adorable. The little bunny.

AUGIE

Thanks — thanks —

MC CRACKEN

(*Eyes bags, coming in*)

Going somewhere?

AUGIE

No — no! Those are my wife's.

MC CRACKEN

Is *she* going somewhere?

AUGIE

No! She's not going anywhere. Just — just some stuff she's taking down to the Community Center — bundles for the poor —

MC CRACKEN
(*Nods*)

Oh, I see.

AUGIE

She's on every committee in Westport — very civic-minded.

MC CRACKEN

I should think the baby would be a full-time job, Mr. Poole.

AUGIE
(*Quickly*)

Oh, he is! She's with him practically every second. Just once a year she likes to do something for the poor.

MC CRACKEN
(*Crossing to bench*)

He certainly *looks* the picture of health.
(*She picks up photo from bench*)

Ahh, the little cherub.
(*She sits on bench*)

And how are you two adjusting to family life?

AUGIE

Oh, fine — just fine!

MC CRACKEN

Because at Rock-a-bye we realize there are many stresses and strains — I mean with a baby in the house.

AUGIE

No stresses and strains around here.

MC CRACKEN

I'm glad to hear it. However, you're what we call "probationary parents" for the first year, until the adoption becomes final.

AUGIE
(*Nervously*)

Yes, yes — I know —
(*Taxi horn sounds outside*)
Well, it was nice of you to drop in, Miss McCracken. Drop in any time.

MC CRACKEN

Thank you, but I'd like to see Mrs. Poole before I go.

AUGIE

Well — well, the fact is — Mrs. Poole isn't feeling very well — the baby kept her up all night.

MC CRACKEN

(*Looking at him, beginning to be suspicious for the first time*)
I thought she was taking these things down to the Community Center?

AUGIE

Oh, she is! She is! Later. When she feels better —
(*Taxi horn sounds again*)

MC CRACKEN

(*Looks out suspiciously*)
There's a taxi waiting for someone, Mr. Poole.

AUGIE

Probably a mistake. Can't be for us — we've got a car.
(*Calls out door*)
We didn't call for a cab! You've got the wrong house, Jack!
(*He comes back and looks at her with a false smile. She is eyeing him very strangely*)

MC CRACKEN

(*Rising*)
Mr. Poole, I must insist on seeing your wife — for a moment, anyway.

AUGIE

Yeah — sure — I'll go get her. Maybe I'd better take these things inside.
(*He picks up both bags. Releases catch on overnight bag. It opens and a fur piece falls out. They both stare at it for a moment*)

MC CRACKEN

I suppose you were taking *that* down to the poor?

AUGIE

We have a higher standard of living in Westport.
(*Repacks bag and places both at end of bench*)

MC CRACKEN

(*Sadly*)
Tell me, Mr. Poole, what's going on between you and your wife?

177

Nothing's going on — at the moment.

MC CRACKEN

Please — I'm an old hand at this. I've seen it happen before. You've had a fight, haven't you? Now, what's it all about?

AUGIE

(*Laughs*)

It's so absurd I hate to even talk about it. You see, my wife's a wonderful girl, but she's a little bit of a snob. Old Trenton, New Jersey, aristocracy. Her father went to Lawrenceville and she wants little Augie to go there, too.

MC CRACKEN

Well?

AUGIE

I don't want him to go to a private school. My father went to a public school and so did I. I don't believe in private schools.

MC CRACKEN

You have loads of time to decide that.

AUGIE

No, we've got to enter him right now. Besides, I can't stand these arguments for the next sixteen years.

MC CRACKEN

She couldn't be leaving over a silly thing like that?

AUGIE

(*Laughs*)

Ah, she's high-strung. Every time we have a little squabble, she packs her bags and makes a big brouhaha. But they never get past the front door. In a couple of minutes she'll rush in here, throw her arms around me, and sob, "Augie, you were right! We'll send him to a public school." Then I'll enter him in Lawrenceville and the whole thing will blow over.

MC CRACKEN

Mr. Poole, your lies have been pathetic.

AUGIE

Lies?

MC CRACKEN

Fortunately, the child is still young enough not to be affected by this.
(*She starts to the door and he follows*)

AUGIE

What are you going to do?

MC CRACKEN

I'm going to make a report to the Board.

AUGIE

Please don't make a report yet, Miss McCracken! I love my wife and she loves me. Give me a chance to straighten this out — please!

MC CRACKEN

(*Hesitates*)
It's against all regulations, but I'll hold my report for one week.

AUGIE

Thank you, Miss McCracken. I can't tell you how grateful I am.

MC CRACKEN

I do hope you can patch things up. I really do. Good-by, Mr. Poole.

(*She goes.* ISOLDE *comes in, wearing a hat and carrying gloves. She crosses to the door and looks out*)

ISOLDE

Didn't I hear a taxi?

AUGIE

Yes.

ISOLDE

What did you do with it?

AUGIE

I sent him away.

ISOLDE
(*Angrily*)

I knew it! I knew you'd do something like this!

AUGIE

No, I'm not trying to pull anything! Listen — I'm fighting for our lives — our baby! You — who pride yourself on being so broad-minded and tolerant — you remind me of your mother.

ISOLDE

I resent that!

AUGIE

Oh, yes! You're always attacking her for being narrow-minded and bigoted. Well, what are you being right now?

ISOLDE

Narrow-minded and bigoted like my mother!

AUGIE

What happened to that free spirit from Bennington that I married?

ISOLDE

You happened to it! I'll call another cab!
(*He puts his hand on phone. She stops*)

AUGIE

Isolde — please — give me five minutes —

ISOLDE

This proves what kind of man you are — if I needed proof, which, God knows, I don't. I'll get my own cab.
(*She runs out outside door*)

AUGIE

(*Starts to follow*)
Isolde! Wait! Please!
(*He stares out, frightened. She goes to bicycle leaning against wall outside and takes it off right*)
What are you doing?
(*Runs to door*)
You can't ride that damn bike to the village! Those trucks — the traffic!
(*Bicycle bell rings off right.* AUGIE *yells*)
Look out!

181

(There is a crash and a scream from ISOLDE *offstage, and he runs out. A moment later he reappears supporting her. She's trying to fight free of him)*

ISOLDE

Let go of me, dammit!

AUGIE

(Tenderly, helping her to the bench)
Baby, you might have hurt yourself — be careful —

ISOLDE

Oh, shut up!

AUGIE

You've sprained it! Look, it's swelling already. I'd better call the doctor —
(Puts her shoe in his pocket and crosses to phone)

ISOLDE

No! I don't need a doctor!

AUGIE

(Pours drink)
Better take a drink — you're pale.

ISOLDE

I'm pale with anger!
(He brings her the drink)

AUGIE

Here, drink this. I'll get the tape.
(He forces glass into her hand and goes into bathroom. She does not drink, sets glass on bench)

182

ISOLDE

Don't bother with the tape — you're not going to touch me!
(*She rises and limps*)

AUGIE

(*Comes in*)
What are you doing? Sit down! The worst thing you can do is
stand on it!

ISOLDE

(*Sits on sofa*)
Don't come near me!
(*He crosses to her and kneels at her feet. She kicks at him*)
Go 'way! Go 'way!

AUGIE

(*Grasping her foot firmly*)
You're going to get this taped, whether you like it or not.
(*He starts to tape it*)
And you're going to listen to me whether you like it or not!
Let me begin by saying —
(ISOLDE *starts to talk and sing*)
I love you — I've always loved you — I never loved anybody
else —

ISOLDE

I'm not listening —
(*Puts fingers in her ears and sings loudly*)

"Roll out the barrel, and we'll have a barrel of fun!
Roll out the barrel — "
(She winces)
Ow! What are you doing!

AUGIE

I've got to make it tight if it's going to support you —
(Quickly and desperately as she turns away)
Isolde, listen. That night it happened, I had nothing to do with
it —

ISOLDE

(Scornfully)
You had nothing to *do* with it!

AUGIE

Practically nothing, I mean. I was a captive audience —

ISOLDE

You fool — you driveling fool!
(She turns away once more)

AUGIE

This is the truth — not many men would admit it. I was scared
to death. At that moment there was nothing else I could think of
to *do* —

ISOLDE

I know — she overpowered you.

184

THE TUNNEL OF LOVE

AUGIE

She embarrassed me. It was that night I flunked out of Rock-a-bye, and you wouldn't talk to me. Psychologically, I was ripe. Anyway, we went to dinner. We drove into town. En route she was hungry, so we stopped at a Howard Johnson's. I wasn't hungry, but my stomach was upset. I'd have liked something like a broiled lamb chop. "Could I have a lamb chop?" I asked the waitress. I didn't want much to eat. "I can give you the children's portion, if you like," she said. "In fact, the lamb chop happens to be on our Simple Simon Special." "I'll have that and a bottle of ale. Give me the ale first." "Well, now, I couldn't give you the ale *and* the Simple Simon," she said, "if you're thinking of substituting it for the milk, but if you want to take it on the Simple Simon — "

(*He stops talking and rises slowly*)

As I tell it, I guess it sounds as idiotic to you as it does to me. Isolde, I know there's no excuse for me. I did a terrible thing. But maybe if I hadn't, this wouldn't have happened.

(*He indicates the bassinet. She looks down at her hands*)

Whatever has happened hasn't changed my love for you. Can't you believe me?

ISOLDE

I want to believe you again, Augie. I want to love you. I don't want to throw away the six years we've had together.

AUGIE

Isolde, maybe you didn't know me as well as you thought you did. I was a frustrated artist and a frustrated man. I couldn't sell my drawings and I couldn't have a child.

185

ISOLDE

Augie — Augie — I don't know how you did it — how you switched it around. But suddenly *I* feel guilty — as if this were all my fault.

AUGIE

Don't blame yourself. It's nobody's fault. I was swept up by a cyclone and deposited in the next county. What good is a marriage that can't stand up under a real jolt?

ISOLDE

Don't talk any more, Augie — please — I can't listen. Where's my shoe?
    (*He takes it out of his pocket, kneels beside her and puts it on.*)
I have such an empty feeling.

AUGIE

Maybe you're hungry. I'm starving myself.
    (*He rises*)
I'll make something.

ISOLDE

There's nothing in the house but milk and Pablum.

AUGIE

Okay. I'll run into the village. What'll I get?

ISOLDE

Will you stop at the Shanghai Gardens and get me a double order of moo-goo-gai-pan?
    (*She dabs at nose with handkerchief*)

AUGIE

Sure! Sure!
(*He starts to door, stops, turns slowly*)
Moo-goo-gai-pan?

ISOLDE

Yes. I've had an irrepressible longing for it all week.

AUGIE

(*Kneeling at sofa*)
What are your *other* symptoms?

ISOLDE

Symptoms? What symptoms? I'm *starved*, that's all!

AUGIE

(*Bubbling over*)
They told us this usually happens when you adopt one! Darling,
I've got a feeling little Augie's going to have a sibling!

ISOLDE

(*Gasps, rising*)

Augie!

AUGIE

(*Embraces her*)
Listen, darling — let's put this damn house on the market and
move back to the city. The country's no place to bring up kids.
Our baby's going to be born in Manhattan — in a normal, *healthy*
atmosphere! And this time I hope to God it looks like you!
(*She laughs and embraces him as —*)

CURTAIN FALLS

187